We Shall Not Fail

We Shall Not Fail

The Inspiring Leadership of

WINSTON CHURCHILL

CELIA SANDYS

and

JONATHAN LITTMAN

PORTFOLIO

PORTFOLIO
Published by the Penguin Group
Penguin Group (USA) Inc., 375 Hudson Street, New York, New York 10014, U.S.A.
Penguin Books Ltd, 80 Strand, London WC2R 0RL, England
Penguin Books Australia Ltd, 250 Camberwell Road, Camberwell, Victoria 3124, Australia
Penguin Books Canada Ltd, 10 Alcorn Avenue, Toronto, Ontario, Canada M4V 3B2
Penguin Books India (P) Ltd, 11 Community Centre, Panchsheel Park,
    New Delhi—110 017, India
Penguin Books (N.Z.) Ltd, Cnr Rosedale and Airborne Roads,Albany, Auckland,
    New Zealand
Penguin Books (South Africa) (Pty) Ltd, 24 Sturdee Avenue, Rosebank, Johannesburg
    2196, South Africa

Penguin Books Ltd, Registered Offices: 80 Strand, London WCZR 0RL, England

First published in 2003 by Portfolio, a member of Penguin Group (USA) Inc.

10 9 8 7 6 5 4 3 2 1

Library of Congress Cataloging-in-Publication Data

Sandys, Celia.
  We shall not fail : the inspiring leadership of Winston Churchill /
Celia Sandys and Jonathan Littman.
      p. cm.
  Includes index.
  ISBN 1-59184-015-5
  1. Churchill, Winston, Sir, 1874–1965. 2. Churchill, Winston, Sir, 1874–1965—
Views on leadership. 3. Great Britain—Politics and government—20th century.
4. Prime ministers—Great Britain—Biography. 5. Leadership. I. Littman, Jonathan,
1958– II. Title.

DA566.9.C5 S266 2003
941.084'092—dc21
[B]   2002192679

This book is printed on acid-free paper. ∞

Printed in the United States of America
Set in Giovanni

FOR ALL WHO ASPIRE TO LEAD.

Contents

List of Illustrations

Chronology

1874   Born November 30 at Blenheim Palace

1895   Commissioned into 4th Hussars

1897   In combat on North-West Frontier of India

1898   Rode in the last great British cavalry charge at Omdurman in the Sudan

1899   South African war correspondent. Captured, escaped, and temporarily rejoined the army

1900   Returned to England and was elected to Parliament

1905   Parliamentary Under-Secretary for the Colonies

1908   Married Clementine Hozier. President of the Board of Trade

1910–11 Home Secretary

1911–15 First Lord of the Admiralty

1915   Resigned from cabinet after Dardanelles disaster. Rejoined army and commanded a battalion in France.

1916   Resigned commission; returned to politics

1917–18 Minister of Munitions

1919–21 Secretary of State for War and Air

1921–22 Colonial Secretary

1924–29 Chancellor of the Exchequer

1930–39 Wilderness years. Led anti-appeasement campaign as backbench member of Parliament.

1939–40 First Lord of the Admiralty

1940–45 Prime Minister

1945   Victory in Europe. Resigned as Prime Minister

1946   Order of Merit. "Iron Curtain" speech in Fulton, Missouri

1951–55 Prime Minister

1953   Knight of the Garter. Nobel Prize in Literature

1965   Died January 24 in London

Introduction

"When did you realize that your grandfather was a great man?"

This is a question I am often asked and one that I find impossible to answer.

I only knew one of my grandfathers and quite naturally assumed that he was like any other grandfather. I never gave it much thought, but if I had to describe a grandfather he would have been a loving and much-loved man, dressed in a siren suit, puffing a huge cigar, with everyone—secretaries, colleagues, friends, and family—running around trying to make his life as comfortable and easy as possible.

He was a man who seemed to have endless knowledge and interests, who recited poetry, made people laugh; and loved animals, walking around his garden at Chartwell, and above all, painting.

One day a present arrived with the message: "Please look after him for me, Your Loving Grandpapa."

In feverish excitement I unwrapped a strangely shaped parcel and found inside a lifesize toy bulldog with a head that moved from side to side when it was pulled along on the wheels set into its paws. My mother explained that someone had sent this to grandpapa and he thought that I might like it. I did but wanted to know why anyone would send him a toy dog. Armed with the explanation that during the war he had been described as a bulldog I set off for school determined to find out what sort of dogs my friends had for grandfathers!

Little by little it dawned on me that there was something very special about my mother's father with whom we spent a lot of time while we were growing up.

Part of this was a gradual realization that other people regarded and treated him as though he were some kind of god. They talked to him and about him in a very special way. As I grew up, he grew old and it was about this time that I began to understand how much he had done for his country and the world.

A year before the terrible events of September 11, I had decided to write this book. I had the good fortune to meet Jonathan Littman, and we decided to form an Anglo-American alliance.

We believe that the legacy of Winston Churchill as an inspiring example of leadership is as relevant today as it was sixty years ago. This was borne out in the aftermath of September 11 when the speeches of both President Bush and Prime Minister Blair took inspiration from his famous wartime speeches. Mayor Rudolph Giuliani said: "Winston Churchill is my great hero. I modeled myself on him. He helped me a lot before, during, and after [the attacks]." There were notices in New York shop windows repeating his advice to the boys of Harrow, his old school, after it had been bombed in 1940: "Never, never give in."

For two weeks following the terrorist attacks The Churchill Center was kept busy attributing Churchill quotations for everyone from the White House staff to the *New York Times*.

Winston Churchill was like every one of us, a unique person. He was above all a very human man who lived life to the full and enjoyed everything he did. A man who believed in truth, courage, and loyalty.

He was not afraid to show his emotions. Anyone who is old enough to remember will recall exactly where they were on the day President Kennedy died. I was with my grandfather in his London house. I had never seen him watch television before, but on that day it was firmly placed on the dining room table and we watched as the tragic story unfolded before our eyes. Tears poured down his face as the news came that the young president was dead, and once more when we watched his beautiful widow, still dressed in her blood-stained clothes, witnessing the swearing in of the new president.

I soon realized that I must treasure these moments when I had to myself the man the whole world thought they owned.

I am lucky to have known and loved Winston Churchill. I hope that in this book you, too, will discover the qualities which made him great.

Any present or future leader can learn and find inspiration from his example.

Celia Sandys

We Shall Not Fail

CHAPTER 1

Be Courageous

Courage is rightly esteemed the first of human qualities because it is the quality which guarantees all others.

—Winston Churchill, *Great Contemporaries*, 1937

A number of men might have come forward to lead Britain in the spring of 1940. Most of the candidates had shunned Winston Churchill for years. Yet when defeat stared Britain in the face, it was to him that the nation turned. Why?

For one thing, he understood war from top to bottom—as a journalist, a soldier, a field commander, and an administrator. He knew how armies worked, and knew the factors that helped them win.

For another, his knowledge fed his innate optimism—and he knew how to communicate both. When he said it was possible to defeat the Nazi juggernaut, the people believed him.

The outlook was bleak. The Nazis were running over France, Belgium, and Holland. Joseph P. Kennedy, the American ambassador in London, told Washington that Britain was finished.

But on May 10, as he assumed the crucial position of wartime Prime Minister, Churchill felt no fear. Instead, he wrote, he became "conscious of a profound sense of relief. At last I had the authority to give directions over the whole scene."

How is that possible? How could any man feel so prepared for such a monumental task?

The short answer is that he had spent his entire life preparing to lead. But how did he prepare? And once in position, how did he lead? We'll take a close look at his mettle and his methods—at the qualities that made him a great leader just when the world required greatness. There was only one Winston Churchill. But the lessons of his challenging life offer modern leaders a treasure to draw on.

We begin with that most precious commodity: courage. Churchill was clearly a man of extraordinary valor. There are a hundred examples of his courage, but General Douglas MacArthur struck on one—the arduous flights Churchill took during the war to Russia, to shore up the crucial alliance with Stalin. "If disposal of all the Allied decorations were today placed by Providence in my hands, my first act would be to award the Victoria Cross to Winston Churchill," said the general. "Not one of those who wear it deserves it more than he. A flight of 10,000 miles through hostile and foreign skies may be the duty of young pilots, but for a Statesman burdened with the world's cares it is an act of inspiring gallantry and valor."

From his earliest days Churchill had worked to develop his reserves of courage. Throughout his life, he chose experiences for their ability to steel, and show, his will.

A successful life in business requires more courage than most people imagine. Executives must routinely resolve crises. An important subordinate may challenge your authority or threaten to quit. You might have to confront someone whose performance is lacking, or take a leap of faith on a new market. Larry Bossidy and Ram Charan write of the central role of courage in their book, *Execution: The Discipline of Getting Things Done.* "Everyone pays lip service to the idea that leading an organization requires strength of character. In execution it's

CHURCHILL THE WARRIOR

Always keen to join the action, even in the most dangerous circumstance, Churchill proved himself a dedicated warrior.

Cuba, 1885. Observer with Spanish forces in guerrilla war.

India, North-West frontier, 1897. Young officer in tribal war.

Sudan, 1898. Fights in cavalry charge during Battle of Omdurman.

South Africa, 1899–1900. Boer War correspondent. Distinguishes himself in armored train ambush.

November 15. Captured. (He later escapes.)

December 12. Rejoins army as lieutenant and later distinguishes himself in battles of Spion Kop and Diamond Hill.

Antwerp, September 1914. As First Lord of the Admiralty takes personal charge of defenses.

Western Front, 1915–1916. Commanding Officer 6th Battalion Royal Scots Fusiliers.

absolutely critical. Without what we call emotional fortitude, you can't be honest with yourself, deal honestly with business and organizational realities, or give people forthright assessments. . . . If you can't do these things you can't execute."

Some call it character, others emotional fortitude. Whatever one calls it, the conventional wisdom holds that courage is like creativity—one either has it or lacks it. You can't build courage as you would build a muscle, can you?

Churchill decided that he could. And he needed to do so, for circumstances had given him a steep mountain to climb. His gifted father harped on his inferior school marks. His beautiful mother did not spare enough time to give him the attention he craved. "I loved her dearly," he later wrote, "but at a distance." Frail and sickly as a child, he had a speech impediment.

In the 1890s, the British Empire was still vast, and its people still celebrated war as a noble undertaking. Poor at football and cricket, Churchill learned to excel at sports that translated directly to the battlefield. At Harrow School he became a crack shot in the Rifle Corps. In his final year there, he competed in the national fencing championship for private schools. Boldly attacking bigger, stronger boys, he defeated four opponents to emerge victorious. "Churchill must be congratulated on his success over all his opponents in the fencing line, many of whom must have been much taller and more formidable than himself," announced the school magazine, adding that it was his "quick and dashing attack which quite took his opponents by surprise." At the Royal Military Academy at Sandhurst, he became a talented horseman and, as a young cavalry officer in India, a high-handicap polo player, in the days when skill at equestrian sports was a reflection of military superiority.

Today the fast track in business begins with earning an MBA from a top university or cutting your teeth in a demanding managerial position. In Churchill's age the path to satisfying one's ambition was less clear. Needing to make his name, he displayed verve in combat. "I am more ambitious for a reputation for personal courage," young Winston wrote to his mother "than anything else in the world." Churchill knew he might be killed in battle, but reckoned, "I shall come back afterwards the wiser and the stronger for my gamble."

DARING MORE

Courage is no stranger among leaders. Franklin D. Roosevelt had to face the debilitating onslaught of polio. Andy Grove of Intel had to escape the Nazis as a child and then the Communists as a young man. Churchill considered courage a tangible asset. On the North-West Frontier of India (now part of Pakistan) he was shocked to see British soldiers abandon their wounded officer to the mercy of ruthless tribesmen. The twenty-two-year-old Churchill risked his own life to save the adjutant, holding off the enemy at close quarters with shots from his revolver. He was equally daring with his words, criticizing without fear or favor anything he found deficient, from the behavior of the troops to the atrocious food. Detractors dubbed him a "publicity hound," but Churchill seemed made for war. In a dispatch a general noted with pleasure "the courage and resolution of W.L.S. Churchill, 4th Hussars."

As James MacGregor Burns writes in *Leadership*, "Leaders, whatever their professions of harmony, do not shun conflict; they confront it, exploit it, ultimately embody it." This was certainly true of Churchill. In the outposts of the British Empire, the dashing soldier began to forge the character that would one day enable him to bear the weight of the free world on his shoulders.

"It was a lively day," he wrote of combat in India. "I was personally under fire from 7.30 a.m. to 8.30 p.m. without a stop, though of course it varied. I rode on my grey pony all along the skirmish line when everyone else was lying down in cover. Foolish perhaps, but I play for high stakes and given an audience there is no act too daring or too noble."

Churchill played hard whatever the sport, unshakably game

PLAY FOR HIGH STAKES

Churchill's letter to his mother from India, September 19, 1897.

> I am very gratified to hear that my follies have not been altogether unnoticed. To ride a grey pony along askirmish line - is not a common experience. But I had to play for high stakes and have been lucky twice,

despite the hazards. He kept up steeplechasing even after serious falls, writing frankly to his brother, Jack, "There is no doubt about it being dangerous." To his mother, on the other hand, he minimized the risks: "I think that you take a rather extreme view of steeplechasing when you call it at once idiotic and fatal."

A severe shoulder injury should have ended his days as a polo player but, with his arm supported by a specially devised sling, he remained a member of the team that won the Indian Inter-Regimental Tournament. Churchill struck three of his team's four goals. To him it was more than a game. His personal style showed in his hard-riding, risk-taking decisiveness. Patrick Thompson, one of his contemporaries, wrote of Winston: "He rides in the game like heavy cavalry getting into position for the assault. He trots about, keenly watching, biding his time, a master of tactics and strategy. Abruptly he sees his chance, and he gathers his pony and charges in, neither deft nor graceful, but full of tearing physical energy—and skilful with it, too. He bears down opposition by the weight of his dash and strikes the ball. Did I say strikes? He slashes the ball."

Proving courage under fire is something one does over time, in many different arenas. Think about how you might improve your reputation for courage, and start taking action.

Resourceful and instinctive, Churchill fought as he played. In 1898 at Omdurman, Churchill was at the head of his troop as the 21st Lancers charged into several thousand Dervish warriors. His bad shoulder made wielding a sword impossible. He drew his Mauser pistol instead, killing three and wounding more. Had his shoulder been sound, he said later, he might well have gone down with his sword. From this experience came his stoic maxim: "One must never forget, when misfortunes come, that it is quite possible they are saving one from something much worse."

In South Africa, in the Boer War, Churchill found a conflict equal to his burgeoning ambition. Within a fortnight of arriving there in 1899 he accompanied an armored train on a reconnaissance. Just two hours down the track the Boers lay in ambush. As it rounded a hill, the train came under fire. The engineer poured on the steam to escape, but a boulder on the track derailed the leading wagons. Several British officers were present, but it was Churchill the war correspondent who took charge. With the improbable assertion that no man is wounded twice in one day, he persuaded the wounded engineer to return to his cab. Under a hail of bullets and artillery fire, he inspired volunteers to leave the shelter of the wagons and work at clearing the wreckage.

The battle lasted an hour, with Churchill, in the words of a private, "walking about in it all as coolly as if nothing was going on." With the wreckage cleared, the locomotive was loaded with wounded and driven to safety under Churchill's command. Returning on foot, in the hope of leading more men to safety, he found they had surrendered. Unarmed, he, too, was captured. A wounded officer described Churchill's conduct "as that of as brave a man as could be found."

The lesson is clear. The next time a crisis erupts, take action instead of waiting for someone or something to come to the rescue. Leadership waits for no one.

After four weeks' imprisonment in Pretoria, Churchill scrambled over the wall and made off into the night. He jumped a freight train then walked for miles across the veld. He was hidden underground by friendly miners and then among bales of wool in a railway wagon bound for Portuguese East Africa. A fortnight after climbing the wall he was back with the army, a few yards from where he had been captured less than six weeks before.

These deeds made him an international hero. Churchill could easily have ridden his reputation to political success. Instead he soldiered on. Within two weeks of his dramatic escape, he was back in action. "I do not know whether I shall see the end or not, but I am quite certain that I will not leave Africa till the matter is settled," he wrote to his sweetheart, Pamela Plowden, who fretted for his safety. "I should forfeit

WANTED DEAD OR ALIVE

Churchill was a wanted man after his escape from a Boer prison camp in South Africa in December of 1899.

£25.—.—

(vijf en twintig pond stg.)
belooning uitgeloofd door
de Sub-Commissie van Wijk V
voor den Specialen Constabel
dezer wijk, die den ontvluchte
Krijgsgevangene
Churchill
levend of dood te dezer kantore
aflevert.—

Namens de Sub-Comm.
Wijk V
D. de Haas
Sec.

Translation.

£25

(Twenty-five Pounds stg.) REWARD is offered by the Sub-Commission of the fifth division, on behalf of the Special Constable of the said division, to anyone who brings the escaped prisoner of war

CHURCHILL,

dead or alive to this office.

For the Sub-Commission of the fifth division,
(Signed) LODK. de HAAS, Sec.

NOTE.-The Original Reward for the arrest of Winston Churchill on his escape from Pretoria, posted on the Government House at Pretoria, brought to England by the Hon. Henry Masham, and is now the property of W. R. Burton.

my self-respect forever if I tried to shield myself behind an easily obtained reputation for courage." Leaders make certain that
their integrity can never be questioned.

The year was 1900. The celebrated journalist was now a
lieutenant in an irregular regiment, the South African Light
Horse. Again he showed striking initiative. Ian Hamilton,
Churchill's commanding officer, wrote in his memoirs, "The
key to the battlefield lay on the summit but nobody knew it
until Winston managed to give me the slip and climb this
mountain. He ensconced himself in a niche not much more
than a pistol shot directly below the Boer commandos. They
could have knocked him off his perch with a volley of stones.
Thus it was from his lofty perch Winston had the nerve to signal me, if I remember right, with a handkerchief on a stick,
that if only I could manage to gallop up at the head of my
mounted infantry we ought to be able to rush the summit."

Curiosity and daring nourish the developing leader. "The
leader wonders about everything, wants to learn as much as he
can, is willing to take risks, experiment, try new things," writes
Warren Bennis in *On Becoming a Leader*. "He does not worry
about failure, but embraces errors, knowing he will learn from
them."

Quite simply, budding leaders move on, change course, and
do not look back. Consider the modern example of Michael
Dell's launching of Dell Computer Corporation. Most would
not dream of starting a business when contemplating medical
school. But premed student Michael Dell spent much of his
first semester at the University of Texas upgrading remain-
dered IBM PCs that he then resold to his fellow students and
businesses, racking up a phenomenal $180,000 in sales his

first month, and leading him to later launch the internationally successful Dell Computer.

Courage in business often requires staking out your line of attack and charging ahead, despite the naysayers. While at Yale, Fred Smith wrote a college paper describing the blueprint for a worldwide overnight delivery company. The paper got only a C, but as we know, that didn't stop the founder of FedEx one bit.

STANDING TALL

Following your passion and telling it like it is seldom make for an easy road to travel. Praised for "conspicuous gallantry" Churchill had his hopes for a decoration dashed by his equally daring journalism. He had upset Lord Roberts, the commander in chief, by his criticism of British military ineptitude in South Africa. His book *The River War* had also questioned Lord Kitchener's inhuman treatment of the enemy after the battle of Omdurman, and Kitchener was now the chief of staff in South Africa. Nevertheless, in spirit Churchill seemed to wear the medal he should have won. Courage under fire became part of his moral and political character. Like Senator John McCain, who bravely endured torture and imprisonment in Vietnam, Churchill emerged from his travails confident and ready for new challenges.

Elected to Parliament on the heels of his Boer War fame, Churchill plunged into politics as he had leaped into battle. He quickly made a name for himself in politics by speaking his mind, even if he was out of step with his own party. It was part of a logical progression. Churchill had been testing his voice since

the age of twenty when he had covered the fight for independence in Cuba as a journalist. By his midtwenties he had become a prolific journalist and confident speaker and had written
five books, including a novel, of which he wrote enthusiastically,
"All my philosophy is put into the mouth of the hero."

Colleagues advised Churchill to go slowly in Parliament, to
find his way before taking unnecessary chances, but caution
was foreign to his character. In his maiden speech in Parliament, Churchill vigorously attacked the government's role in
the Boer War. Though only twenty-six, the former officer had
the audacity to argue, successfully, for economy in army
spending, writing, "A better army does not necessarily mean a
bigger army. There ought to be ways of reforming a business,
other than by merely putting more money into it. There are
more ways of skinning a cat." So, too, did he take a tremendous chance when opposing his party's central policies, arguing for free trade and the end of protectionist tariffs.

The fight over free trade would ultimately lead Churchill to
switch parties, a subject we'll discuss in the following chapter,
Challenge Convention. The path of courage and candor is seldom easy. When Churchill joined the Liberal Party, the doors
of two prestigious London clubs were closed to him. He was
blackballed by the Hurlingham Club and he felt he should resign from the Carlton Club. Principled stands became his signature. He fought for the rights of Jews when many of his
fellow members of Parliament were unabashed anti-Semites.
He proclaimed Chinese indentured labor "an evil inheri-
tance." Later, as Home Secretary, he sought to bring order and
fairness to the criminal justice system.

He was finding his voice and demonstrating his integrity. In
the field of justice, he was not only reforming a system that dis-

proportionately targeted the young and poor, imprisoning many for being unable to pay minor bills. He was also drawing the injustice to the attention of those in power, reminding Parliament that the "treatment of crime and criminals is one of the most unfailing tests of the civilization of any country" and that "there is a treasure, if you can only find it, in the heart of every man—these are the symbols which in the treatment of crime and criminals mark and measure the stored-up strength of a nation."

Churchill's courage became the wild card with which he turned the tables, sometimes changing the opinion of Parliament as he did over the Amritsar incident of 1919. Brigadier General Reginald Dyer had ruthlessly ordered the massacre of unarmed Punjabis who had been protesting against public whippings and an order that they crawl through a street where an Englishwoman had been molested. Nearly four hundred protesters were mowed down by machine gunners. Dyer was forced into retirement, which made him a martyr to the British establishment and gave rise to a debate in Parliament.

Churchill was not prepared to endorse the methods of dictators. Britain could not condone the Amritsar incident any more than it could the "bloody and devastating terrorism" of Bolshevism. "I do not think that it is in the interests of the British Empire or of the British Army for us to take a load of that sort for all time upon our backs. We have to make it absolutely clear, some way or another, that this is not the British way of doing business." To drive home his point he noted that the number of Indian victims was nearly identical to the number of members of Parliament listening to his speech. The motion, which had seemed certain to approve the general's murderous actions, was defeated in Parliament by nearly two to one.

SHARING COURAGE

Churchill's immense courage in World War II played such a large and varied role in his leadership that we will touch on it only briefly here. But it's clear that when Britain had to stand alone Churchill epitomized Britain's courage and resilience. His inspiring words, his energy, his trademark V sign and ever-present cigar all combined to communicate his tremendous courage.

More than a few politicians were ambivalent about working with the often gruff, always controversial Churchill. He had been locked out of government during the long years of appeasement of Nazi Germany in the 1930s. Some wondered whether he was right for the job of wartime Prime Minister. Business leaders face similar crises of confidence when they take over a troubled company or a failing division. Displaying confidence in the face of uncertainty and making hard choices steel your will and reinforce your leadership.

Upon becoming Prime Minister, Churchill gathered his twenty-five ministers together and revealed that he had reflected "whether it was part of my duty to consider entering into negotiations with That Man." He ran through the awful consequences of such a devil's bargain—right down to becoming a Nazi slave state. His words left no doubt about his conviction. "I am convinced that every man of you would rise up and tear me down from my place if I were for one moment to contemplate parley or surrender. If this long island story of ours is to end at last, let it end only when each one of us lies choking in his own blood upon the ground."

That blood-and-guts declaration of resolve won Churchill cheers and enthusiastic claps on the back. Churchill knew that there were members of his Cabinet who still believed appeasement with Hitler was possible, but his warrior's cry consolidated his position, steeling his ministers with his iron will. As he later recounted, "I am sure that every minister was ready to be killed quite soon, and have all his family and possessions destroyed, rather than give in."

Courage is infectious. When air-raid sirens wailed over London, Churchill often clambered up to the roof to watch the fireworks, rather than scurrying down to the shelter. Notwithstanding his age and sometimes precarious health, he dashed around the world through hostile skies and across dangerous waters to meet Stalin and Roosevelt and to visit the various front lines. More than once Churchill tried the patience of his generals by his delight at being close to the action, even when under shellfire. But Churchill felt the need to discover personally how things were going and to share the hazards and adventure of war. He took chances because he knew his actions were inspirational.

By never sidestepping a problem you can engender courage in others. You must calmly face workers that must be let go or a division about to be cut back. You must handle the crisis head-on. You must share the pain. As Churchill explained in his war memoirs, "A man who has to play an effective part in taking, with the highest responsibility, grave and terrible decisions of war may need the refreshment of adventure. He may also need the comfort that when sending so many others to their death he may share in a small way their risks."

RISKING FAILURE

In 1909, while still President of the Board of Trade, Churchill was appointed to the Committee of Imperial Defence and immediately became interested in aviation. He was concerned that the government was not taking the matter seriously. On February 25 he told the committee that the government's aviation proposals might be too amateurish. He advised the committee to "place ourselves in communication with Mr. Orville Wright, and avail ourselves of his knowledge."

Courageous men and women get more done. Churchill's fearless approach to life took him where others failed to tread and his curiosity led to important innovations, as we shall see in Chapter 9, Experiment. He became convinced, for instance, of the military potential of aircraft long before many contemporaries, partly because he was daring enough to venture into the air himself. How could he be knowledgeable about aircraft if he stayed earthbound? Once up in the clouds, he was hooked. No matter that flying in 1912 was arguably more dangerous than riding a space shuttle in 2000, or that Churchill, at thirty-eight, was six years older than the cut-off age for a novice at that time. Churchill set his sights on earning a pilot's license.

He was not particularly gifted, but, as usual, what terrified the average man he found thrilling. He escaped death by the narrowest of margins. "We were scarcely ninety foot above the ground, just the normal height for the usual side-slip fatal accident, the commonest of all," Churchill wrote of a terrifying crash, from which he amazingly emerged with little more than bruises. There were emergency landings. Others were not so lucky. Two of Churchill's instructors died in the very planes in which the future Prime Minister had recently flown. Finally, after pleas from his distraught wife and worried friends, Churchill announced he was quitting.

He looked on the experience as a tonic, good for his nerve, spirits, and virtue. It had made him something of an expert at what he knew would be a critical weapon of war. "I have been up nearly 140 times, with many pilots, & all kinds of machines, so I know the difficulties the dangers & the joys of the air—well enough to appreciate them, & to understand all the questions of policy which will arise in the near future." By seeing things with his own eyes, the First Lord of the Admiralty gained a tremendous understanding of the powers and limitations of flight. Largely because he had used them, Churchill came to believe in the value of instruments in an age when most pilots flew by the seat of their pants. He had a biplane fitted with dual controls that "would be useful for long-distance flying and enable one pilot to relieve the other."

Take time to think creatively about your organization. Where might dual controls help when the going gets rough?

SECOND CHANCES

Courage and boldness give one more than depth. They generate second chances. Think of all the entrepreneurs and company founders who succeeded only after several failures. It is precisely when things go most wrong that you learn the most about yourself. Churchill's years of isolation in the 1930s required tremendous fortitude and resilience to endure. But he had weathered a greater storm nearly twenty years before when domestic politics had made him the scapegoat for the huge military debacle at Gallipoli in World War I. Stripped of his office and offered only a cabinet post with no influence, he resigned from the government. Seldom in Britain's history had such a gifted politician fallen as far and as fast. Many wrote Churchill off as utterly finished.

Let's put this into a modern, civilian perspective. What would a similarly humiliated politician or business executive do today? Most would probably seek some lesser post or retire to academic life. Churchill crossed the Channel to fight in the trenches. He was forty, his dashing days in South Africa more than fifteen years behind him, but he headed to the front with all the enthusiasm of a young patriot. He was most certainly risking his life. Yet this was more than a public penance for those who had died in Gallipoli. He was also starting fresh, seeking nothing less than an emotional and spiritual rejuvenation.

He asked for a command and was at first offered a brigade. A change in commanders in chief reminded him that he was no longer the power he had been. The best he could be offered was a lowly battalion. He grasped it with both hands. His wife and friends worried. The trenches were an ugly, dangerous place. He wrote to Clementine of defences built so haphazardly that the limbs of half-buried corpses could be seen, a hellish muddy stew of dirt and garbage accompanied by the sounds of "rifles & machine guns & the venomous whining & whirring of the bullets which pass overhead."

He reveled at being a small part of a noble cause. He accepted that as a reserve officer he would first have to relearn the ropes before he commanded his own battalion. "I do not know when I have passed a more joyous three weeks. . . . I share the fortunes of a company of Grenadiers. It is a jolly life with nice people; and one does not mind the cold and wet and general discomfort." He was frustrated at being cut off from politics, powerless to influence events of which he believed he had greater understanding than those in command. Near the midpoint of his life and career, Churchill took the greatest of all risks. He swallowed his pride and started over, from the bottom. He somehow sensed that to succeed he must first embrace his failure.

To any leader or executive struggling against long odds, it is a powerful story.

CHURCHILLIAN PRINCIPLES

- Meet challenges head on.
- Be curious and daring. Seek opportunities to display courage in the ordinary course of business or daily life.
- A good leader creates a culture where failure and error are looked upon as steps toward success.
- A demonstration of personal courage can galvanize a team or organization that lacks resolve.
- When life or business deals a bad hand, have faith. The most inspiring opportunities for courage come when you face the longest odds.

CHAPTER 2

Challenge Convention

No idea is so outlandish that it should not be considered with a searching but at the same time a steady eye.

—Winston Churchill, Parliament, May 23, 1940

I t goes without saying that Churchill was unconventional. From his swashbuckling youth, through his long political career, financed by his countless works of history and journalism, Churchill was an original. Who else would regularly dictate memoranda from the bath? He took his cues from no one.

It is one thing to have a unique lifestyle but quite another to carry that philosophy into the direction and organization of government or business. Churchill was an original both in his personal and in his official life. He was the antibureaucrat.

If Churchill were alive today he probably would smile at America's rebellious, skateboarding youth. Lady Violet Bonham-Carter recalled: "When Home Secretary he obdurately refused to prohibit roller-skating on pavements."

Churchill's ambitious goals, unfettered imagination, and willingness to institute courageous and innovative but often unpopular changes meant he would never allow inefficient bureaucracies to slumber on. Leaders today can learn much from how Churchill tackled his many governmental responsibilities. Several times during his wide-ranging career he found himself in a situation similar to that of a CEO hired by a struggling company. More often than not, Churchill had to overcome stubborn resistance to his new programs—resistance

25

that threatened his own credibility. Leaders sometimes have no choice but to take risks.

BEST PRACTICES

Consider, for example, the course Churchill set when he was appointed First Lord of the Admiralty in late 1911. He advocated the creation of a Naval War Staff, to provide much-needed professional direction for the Royal Navy, the largest and most powerful fleet afloat. The professional head of the navy, Admiral Wilson, balked at such a change and, after trying to work with him and finding him too stubborn, Churchill had no alternative but to ask for his resignation. Even with his successor it was by no means plain sailing, for the navy had an institutional fear that a naval staff might breed officers not compatible with those who actually manned ships. But Churchill had no choice. As Jim Collins writes in *Good to Great,* the first step in a leader transforming an organization is "getting the right people on the bus (and the wrong people off the bus)."

Churchill's plan was sound. The army had long since established a War Staff and it was time the navy caught up with modern times. Churchill recognized the increasing complexity of the navy's vessels, weapons, and operations and was stunned to learn that naval officers did not have to "read a single book about naval war, or pass even the most rudimentary examination in naval history." He sensed Britain's navy was not seeing the forest for the trees and later wrote, "We had more captains of ships than captains of war." Therefore he set about developing not just a means of training officers, but a wise and experienced staff that would provide "reasoned opinion" and "guide" the naval policy.

One of Churchill's memoranda at the time, describing the rationale for the War Staff, made it clear that Churchill was advocating nothing less than training in leadership: "The formation of a War Staff does not mean the setting up of new standards of professional merit or the opening of a road of advancement to a different class of officers. It is to be the means of preparing and training those officers who arrive, or are likely to arrive, by the excellence of their sea service at stations of high responsibility, for dealing with the more extended problems which await them there."

Slowly but surely Churchill's Naval War Staff took shape and came to play a major part in modernizing the British navy. Churchill had not only recognized that the navy needed enlightened leadership, but also what managers today often call "best practices." Churchill saw the Naval War Staff as the development of a collective "brain . . . tireless and unceasing in its action, applied continuously to the scientific and speculative study of naval strategy and preparation."

No organizational initiative may be more essential than figuring out how to create leaders. Seventy years after Churchill modernized the Royal Navy, Jack Welch would help to remake General Electric through revitalizing a tired management training center called Crotonville. Welch recognized that his vast organization needed a place to develop both the best leaders and best practices. Indeed Welch seemed to echo Churchill's sentiments when he wrote of GE: "I wanted it focused on leadership development, not specific functional training. I wanted it to be the place to reach the hearts and minds of the company's best people, the inspirational glue that held things together as we changed."

GIVE AN ORGANIZATION WINGS

There must be room for informed instinct. Like all good leaders, Churchill had an instinctive sense of timing when it came to new ideas and methods. Soon after he went to the Admiralty, Churchill thought it only sensible to create the Royal Naval Air Service. It was hard going. The British army was charged with the aerial defense of the nation and the bureaucrats holding the purse strings could not imagine what aircraft had to do with ships. Though the army had the franchise on aviation it had largely squandered that opportunity and viewed aircraft as little more than a means of aerial reconnaissance for land battles.

Churchill was fighting a classic turf battle, in this case, against the army, which was demanding sole responsibility for the air defense it could not provide. Similar struggles happen all the time in business. All too often institutional resistance to change dooms new initiatives. What's the solution? As Bossidy and Charan write in *Execution*, "The leader's personal involvement, understanding and commitment are necessary to overcome this passive (or in many cases 'active') resistance." Churchill understood the critical role of this "personal connection" in making the case for a crucial new initiative. He pressed on, seeing no problem in Britain's fielding two air forces. He correctly foresaw that the Royal Naval Air Service would be needed to protect harbors and stores of fuel, and he also promoted aircraft as aggressive machines of war, pushing the technologies that the army had ignored, such as machine gunnery and bombing.

New ideas often meet resistance and it was only through persistence that Churchill launched his naval air program.

Three times the Treasury rejected his requests before finally funding an Air Department at the Admiralty.

Leaders have to be persistent and optimistic to reinvigorate a somnolent institution. Churchill discovered early on that often the biggest obstacle to improving an organization was the staff's opposition to change. Consider what he faced when reorganizing the Ministry of Munitions in July 1917, his first post after the debacle of the Dardanelles and his self-imposed exile at the front. Churchill's reputation was so low that many expected he would receive a hostile reception when he was introduced to the staff. That did not deter him, recalled Harold Bellman. Churchill began by acknowledging frankly that "he started at scratch in the popularity stakes." He laid out his ambitious plans to increase the flow of munitions. "This was not an apology. It was a challenge," said Bellman. "Those who came to curse remained to cheer."

There's an irony here. Just when your authority seems lowest is often the ideal time to consolidate your leadership.

STREAMLINE AND REVAMP

Once Churchill had begun to win the hearts and minds of the staff, he set out to streamline the workings of the Ministry of Munitions. He reduced fifty separate fiefdoms to twelve. He appointed a Council Secretariat to coordinate the once nearly autonomous departments. He created a Munitions Council to manage the hitherto chaotic competition for vital resources. Churchill also struck an imaginative £100-million trade agreement with the United States.

Top leaders do more than simply streamline and coordinate operations. They infuse an organization with vitality and

FIRST LORD'S MINUTES

Churchill's legendary minutes pressed for new ideas. He wrote thousands during World War I and World War II. These two were written before World War I.

Second Sea Lord.

I am convinced that it is necessary to authorise and organise the direct entry of civilian flyers to the Naval Air Wing. The maximum age should, I think, be higher than 22. I apprehend that the numbers will not be forthcoming unless the age is raised to, say, 24. It is necessary to offer to a man who will give you ten years flying either (*a*) a pension or a lump sum or (*b*) permanent employment. . . .

D.A.D.

I should be glad if one of the Sopwith biplanes at Eastchurch could be fitted with dual controls of exact equality (*i.e.*, without over-riding power), and if the engine switches, gauges, &c., were duplicated too. This machine would be useful for long distance flying and enable one pilot to relieve the other.

Pray let me have an estimate of the time the work would take to execute and the cost involved.

a sense of purpose. Decades before his ideas became popular through the emergence of consultants, Churchill reenergized organizations by his fresh approach. Churchill had a knack for humanizing things and tasks, for turning the dreary into something dynamic. There was more than a little of the child in Churchill, and he often gave the invigorating impression of playing a fascinating new game. Once dull and amorphous departments were named and given initials, X for explosives, D for design, F for finance. Churchill dubbed himself "the Nitrate King."

Stop for a moment. Can you think of names and titles that might enliven your teams or departments?

Churchill revamped communications between departments and, decades before Ronald Reagan preached the virtues of brevity, Churchill insisted that staff minutes be limited to a single page. Once routine tasks were invested with purpose. Churchill introduced the wartime equivalent of business plans, telling the managers responsible, "If you know what your war plan is, it is quite easy to parcel out your material."

This was radical thinking in 1917. So, too, was the following letter, sent only weeks after he became the Minister of Munitions to the management of every steel company in Britain. Churchill may have had the advantage of invoking the war, but today's leaders might learn much from how he invested the most ordinary task with purpose and honor: "The foundation upon which all our chances of Victory stand is Steel. . . . Every man or manager who is engaged in Steel Production is directly engaged in smiting down the enemy and bringing the war to a speedy close. And although he may not share the perils and sufferings of the fighting troops, he can win for himself the right to share their honor when victory is attained."

Nor was Churchill one to leave the achievement of his goals to chance. He discovered at the Ministry of Munitions, as he had earlier at the Admiralty, that contractors would sometimes book orders and fill them when they pleased. That may have been the routine in peacetime, but Churchill would not tolerate it in war. Churchill arranged for meetings with the contractors themselves at his office, where he got firm commitments for the production of armaments and ships.

Yet Churchill was modern and unconventional enough to recognize that even during the war, all work and no play was not the way to accelerate the production of armaments. He needed the dedication of factory workers to achieve the necessary targets, but sensed correctly that he would not earn this by pushing them too hard. "I am in principle strongly opposed to Sunday work, except in emergencies," he wrote to one of his staff members. "It usually results in workmen receiving double wages for working on Sunday, and taking Monday off."

The next time your team or company is facing a deadline, leave room for breaks and recreation. You'll be surprised at how fast and how well the work will get done.

BE PRAGMATIC

Churchill's approach to resolving labor disputes and inspiring management was equally unconventional. He cared little for rules or appearances when his goals were threatened. He made the tough decisions over which so many businessmen and politicians waffle. Churchill took control of a strikebound factory in the name of the government, though that had never been done before. When munitions workers walked out at several factories, he threatened to draft them into the army. Remarkably, through it all Churchill won the allegiance of thousands of workers. He may have been tough about strikes, but he was extraordinarily fair when it came to wages, introducing higher wages for skilled workers, who hitherto were being paid only half as much as those doing piecework. Later, when visiting the front line, Churchill made personal appeals by telegraph to workers back in Britain, encouraging increased production levels to remedy particular shortages.

Churchill's detractors have called him an opportunist, as if it were wrong to seize opportunities. But he was really a pragmatist. Churchill left the Conservative Party early in his career because he was out of tune with its policies. Though he joined the Liberals on the issue of free trade he was also putting himself at the center of a rising party that was embracing a host of issues critical to social progress. Churchill was not and never would be a party man. Much later in his career, when the Liberal Party lost its drive and vision, Churchill returned to the Conservative Party.

Wise leaders do not stick blindly to fixed positions when conditions change. Many companies, for example, oppose layoffs on principle, but when times are rough if they do not reduce their workforce they risk the viability of the entire enterprise.

Churchill was a roll-up-your-sleeves-style leader, and it was this sort of everyday pragmatism that made him valuable in solving a crisis or in tackling the unexpected. Churchill was not one to fall for slogans or to become a slave to ideology. He believed in certain principles, such as justice, democracy, free enterprise, and free trade. But during a crisis he could make the difficult judgments needed in the interests of Britain. This nuts-and-bolts approach gave Churchill a flexibility that modern leaders would do well to study. Always reserve for yourself the right to change your mind, to switch course in light of changing events and conditions: "The only way a man can remain consistent during changing circumstances is to change with them while preserving the same dominating purpose." To abandon the old policy, Churchill noted, it is often necessary to adopt the new.

Shortly after joining the Liberal Party, Churchill was confronted while electioneering with a leaflet listing his past criticisms of his new party. In true Churchillian style, he tackled the hecklers head-on with a candor that rings out over the intervening century as virtually unique among politicians: "I said a lot of stupid things when I worked with the Conservative Party, and I left it because I did not want to go on saying stupid things." Then, in a dramatic flourish, he tore the paper to shreds.

FIGHT TRENCH THINKING

Throughout World War I Churchill challenged the Prime Minister, the Cabinet, and the military to rise above the strategic and intellectual rut so many of them had fallen into. There is a paralysis that often grips an organization stuck with a failing strategy. A true leader, however, must back new initiatives, despite the gulf in ideas and attitudes that often exists between the establishment and the leader. For example, many of Churchill's contemporaries in government despaired that the pattern of bloody trench warfare, which dominated strategic thinking, made victory impossible. Churchill, in contrast, frequently seemed invigorated by the challenge.

Experts are less likely to challenge convention than perceptive amateurs. Though not an expert in military technology, Churchill possessed something far more valuable, a curiosity and fertile imagination that would carry him beyond the most ardent skeptics. The War Office resented many of Churchill's early military ideas and rejected them out of hand. He was, after all, First Lord of the Admiralty and in no way responsible for the War Office, that is, army, policy. His engaging ideas ranged from fitting a metal shield to a caterpillar tractor to his "attack by the spade,"—digging hundreds of intersecting tunnels behind enemy lines.

Leaders know that you must entertain lots of fanciful ideas to land one that succeeds. Churchill kept tinkering with his most promising conception, ordering Rolls-Royce vehicles to be fitted with armor plate, and visualizing the use of planking to cross trenches. When an army officer thought the idea promising, Churchill suggested to the Prime Minister that an experiment should be begun to "fit up a number of steam tractors with small armored shelters, in which men and machine guns could be placed, which would be bullet-proof." Caterpillar tracks would make trench crossing possible. The War Office turned the idea down, but Churchill persisted. The Admiralty designed a caterpillar-driven land ship code-named "tank." The War Office prophesied it would be mired in the mud of the Western Front. Detractors called it Winston's Folly.

Of course, Churchill was startlingly correct about the future of the tank. He saw tanks as an essential part of the constellation of weapons needed to win the war, using technology to vastly increase the offensive capability of the army. Unfortunately, in 1916 no one else had the vision to dream up the tactics to make best use of the new technology and Churchill's ideas went unheeded. On September 16, the day after the first tanks went into action on the Somme, he wrote to Admiral Fisher, "My poor land battleships have been let off prematurely and on a petty scale. In that idea resided one real victory." The element of surprise had been lost and in reply to a letter from the historian and novelist Arthur Conan Doyle Churchill opined, that it would have made better military sense to have held them back for later use in greater numbers. "The caterpillars [tanks] are the land sisters of the monitors [a type of warship]. The monitor was the beginning of the torpedo-proof fleet. *Surprise* was the true setting for them both."

Later, as Minister of Munitions, Churchill created a Tank Board to begin production on a large scale. His vision would not be fully implemented until World War II, but he had correctly foreseen that tanks would be far more than another form of bombardment "but an indispensable adjunct to infantry."

It's that kind of imagination and drive that separates the great from the merely good. Try thinking about how you might encourage people to dream up the next critical tool for your organization. Be ready for detractors. One of the most important steps in innovation is to overcome the naysayers who don't fully understand the potential of new technology.

Indeed, Churchill's willingness to question traditional thinking on everything from trench warfare to military technology demonstrates an essential quality of organizational leadership. To reform and reorganize are only the first steps in making an organization or company more productive. The greatest factor in rejuvenation is rekindling the individual and collective imagination of an organization. As Collins exhorts in

Good to Great, "Lead with questions, not answers." Churchill was a leader who inspired people and organizations to think about the means of winning a war. His ideas raised the level of work and achievement of thousands of men and women. It seemed nothing could stop him from searching for a solution to a difficult problem. When the United States suddenly cut short the production of steel it was sending to Britain for the manufacture of shells, Churchill was not short of novel solutions, suggesting everything from collecting the iron railings from the public parks and streets to removing the steel from unfinished buildings and gathering the spent shells on yesterday's battlefields. Sometimes these ideas were not practical, but his energy, purpose, and drive were contagious. Impressed by Churchill's achievements at the Ministry of Munitions, Leo Amery, a member of Parliament who would be a minister in Churchill's World War II government, wrote, "Whatever his defects may be, there is all the difference in the world between the tackling of a big problem like this by a man of real brain and imagination, and its handling by good second rate men like [Generals] Robertson and Haig, who still live in the intellectual trench in which they have been fighting."

Early in World War II, when he was again First Lord of the Admiralty, Churchill questioned the need for a complete blackout. He suggested an imaginative system of central electrical switching in towns and cities so that the streetlights could be left on "for people going to cinemas and theatres" but switched off when an air raid was threatened. Technically it proved impractical, but it is another example of the fresh approach he brought to tired thinking.

LEARN FROM MISTAKES

Challenge convention and you're bound to make mistakes. It is the price of success. The line between winning and losing in war or business can be slim and may ride on variables beyond your control. Just as today's leaders can learn much from Churchill's successes, it is important to examine what happened when things went wrong. The disastrous Dardanelles campaign during World War I was a political setback from which few thought Churchill would ever recover. It's a rich example of how even the most stalwart leader can sometimes reach too far.

As 1914 drew to a close a stalemate gripped the Western Front, with both sides entrenched from the North Sea to Switzerland. Churchill suggested a naval incursion into the Baltic and a linkup with the Russians to break the deadlock. Then came a request from Russia for action in the Dardanelles. Lord Kitchener, Secretary of State for War, pressed the issue by asking Churchill if a naval bombardment could be made there. Churchill said a naval attack would be ineffectual but a combined military and naval assault would be another matter. Though Kitchener said he would make no troops available, he still thought that naval action might deter Turkey from sending reinforcements to the Russian front.

The Russian appeal could not go unanswered and it was left to Churchill to take up the very plan about which he had serious doubts. He telegraphed Admiral Carden, then blockading the Dardanelles, for his views. Back came the surprising reply that the Dardanelles might be forced and a squadron established in the Sea of Marmara, leaving Constantinople (now Istanbul) at Britain's mercy.

Churchill swung into action. Prime Minister Herbert Asquith and the War Council endorsed the plan, while Kitchener now offered to provide the necessary troops. Then, on the very day the naval bombardment of the Turkish forts began, Kitchener severely reduced his offer, saying the troops might be needed in France. Churchill lacked the authority to order enough troops but placed on record his dissension. If a disaster occurred on account of lack of troops he could disclaim all responsibility.

A less intrepid leader than Churchill might have advocated abandoning the campaign when Kitchener reneged on his first offer of troops. But as Churchill himself said of the Dardanelles, "You cannot win this war by sitting still." Churchill knew that even without ground troops it was a legitimate gamble. Eventually, but far too late, thousands of troops were supplied for what became known as the Gallipoli campaign. Tragically, the operation came to resemble the intractable stalemate it had sought to break. In less than a year more than 250,000 troops were lost without any gain in enemy territory.

Largely for political reasons Churchill became the scapegoat for this military disaster. This was unjust but Churchill did learn from his experience and contemporary leaders should remember the important lesson: When running risks, responsibility must be matched by authority. Churchill had taken a tremendous risk by advocating and attempting to implement a complicated plan without the authority to fully coordinate its implementation. A quarter of a century later, on the day he became Prime Minister during World War II, he instituted a proper organization for coordinated war planning.

Well-taken risks characterize successful organizations. But when the execution of a novel plan slips beyond the control and management of a leader, risks multiply. Over time, leaders discover the critical elements that need to be in place to implement challenging or unconventional plans. They also recognize that indecision is not the path to leadership. Sometimes the odds are good and sometimes they are long. Learning from one's own mistakes and those of others provides a helpful background. But it is up to every leader to judge when a particular risk is worth taking.

CHURCHILLIAN PRINCIPLES

- When new problems arise consider creating new organizations or methods for solving them.
- Refurbish rusty organizations. Streamline them to create clear lines of coordination and command.
- Infuse ordinary tasks with purpose by humanizing them, adding an element of fun and removing bureaucracy.
- All work and no play makes Jack a dull boy. Excessive workloads reduce creativity and lower production. Provide time for relaxation, no matter how tight the deadline.
- Be pragmatic and flexible. Change rules and policies when the situation demands it. Keep an open mind.
- Inspire people to find quicker ways of achieving goals.
- Make sure technology is not spurned by those who do not understand it.
- Learn from your mistakes. One of the biggest lessons is recognizing how many variables you can juggle and expect to succeed.

CHAPTER 3

On Speaking and Writing

Of all the talents bestowed upon men, none is so precious as the gift of oratory. . . . He who enjoys it wields a power more durable than a great king. He is an independent force in the world. Abandoned by his party, betrayed by his friends, stripped of his offices, whoever can command this power is still formidable.

—Winston Churchill, "The Scaffolding of Rhetoric," 1898

From his soaring speeches and inspirational BBC broadcasts to his daring journalism as a young wartime correspondent, Churchill was a master communicator. He did far more than simply raise the spirits of the British and the Allies during the war. Few authors, public speakers, or journalists can point to more popular and literary success than that of Winston Churchill. He was one of the most highly paid, best read authors and journalists of the twentieth century. He won the Nobel Prize in literature.

Perhaps more than any modern figure Churchill demonstrated how communication skills set a leader apart from the pack. Though few may equal his verbal mastery, Churchill's accomplishments are worth studying because so much of what he achieved came through hard work and innovative approaches. Early in his career he developed elaborate methods for preparing speeches and producing everything from simple memos to multivolume histories. Churchill's techniques of research and dictation are especially relevant for today's time-crunched executives.

Churchill's elegant language, piercing wit, and knack for hitting upon a rhythmical yet simple phrase to pay homage or inspire are what come immediately to mind when we think of Churchill the Communicator. Phrases like, "Give us the tools and we will finish the job," and "men will say, "This was their finest hour.'" are among his well-known sayings. But what truly distinguished him as a speaker and writer was his over-riding sense of purpose and his ability to uplift, persuade, and tug at the heartstrings. Whether he was broadcasting or dictating a memo, Churchill always had a specific goal in mind.

What makes Churchill's legacy all the more pertinent for leaders today is that he was largely self-taught. In other words you do not have to graduate from Harvard or Oxford to become proficient on the podium and with the pen.

THE CHURCHILL CANON

Before delving into Churchill's methods it is worth taking stock of his phenomenal achievements: forty-four books, some eight hundred full-scale articles, many other smaller pieces and even a screenplay on Napoleon, albeit unfinished, written at the suggestion of Charlie Chaplin. Churchill's speeches number in the thousands (eighteen volumes were published); his memos, often literary masterpieces in themselves, in the tens of thousands. On top of this, Churchill dictated an amazing daily torrent of letters at home, at his office, at sea, and in the air. In one year alone, on one subject, his compelling history of his great ancestor, the first Duke of Marlborough, he dictated more than three hundred letters. In all it was an incredible output.

Churchill built his confidence and furthered his political

career not only by the force of his words, but by making sure he was well paid for his efforts (a lesson leaders such as Colin Powell and Jack Welch have learned). He was earning his living and ensuring he could support the lifestyle his political ambition demanded. At the age of twenty-five Churchill's reputation as an author and correspondent brought him a lucrative deal with the *Morning Post* to cover the Boer War. Paid £250 a month (the equivalent of a modern annual salary of $240,000) he became the most highly paid correspondent of the day. He continued in similar style, thirty years later commanding an advance in today's money of $450,000 for his biography of Marlborough, with U.S. and serial rights bringing in as much again. *A History of the English-Speaking Peoples* was equally lucrative, while his six-volume history of World War II sold hundreds of thousands of copies.

One of the central lessons that Churchill the Communicator teaches leaders is to strike when the voice or pen is hot. Churchill seized opportunities. The triumphant twenty-five-year-old national hero returned from South Africa to embark on lecture tours throughout Britain and America. In one frenetic month alone he hustled around Britain, from one packed hall to another, earning about $300,000 in today's currency.

But for all his talents, it is a mistake to think that Churchill rose to such heights without hard work. Few businessmen and politicians become versatile writers and speakers overnight. Even speakers who seem to have the most natural gifts have often labored long and hard to hone their skills. Whether they come by their skills naturally or through hard work, the best public speakers share a common trait. They take seriously the fundamental lesson passed on by Churchill, John F. Kennedy, and other great leaders. They never end a speech without asking their audience to rise to an occasion or to meet a challenge.

BECOMING A SPEAKER

Becoming a solid public speaker, or writer for that matter, is rarely achieved through formal education or by following the rules. Like many talented figures, Churchill rejected the school syllabus. He spurned what bored him: mathematics, Latin, and the classics. His housemaster at Harrow, writing to Lady Randolph, reported, "Winston has got worse. Constantly late for school, losing his books, he is so regular in his irregularity that I really don't know what to do. If he is unable to conquer his slovenliness he will never make a success of school. As far as ability goes he ought to be at the top of his form, whereas he is at the bottom." Churchill seemed destined to become, in his father's words, "a mere social wastrel."

Young Winston's disdain for Latin and the classics led him to be packed off to remedial English. Fortunately, his teacher had an imaginative teaching method: he coded each element in a sentence with a unique color, helping the students to quickly identify subjects, objects, and even conjunctive clauses. Leaders fashion diamonds out of coal, turning apparent failures into successes. Churchill was no different. Through constant repetition of his teacher's gymnastics in grammar, he later wrote, "I learned it thoroughly. Thus I got into my bones the essential structure of the ordinary British sentence, which is a noble thing. And when after years my schoolfellows who had won prizes for writing such beautiful Latin poetry and pithy Greek epigrams had to come down again to common English, to earn their living or make their way, I did not feel myself at any disadvantage."

The lesson for modern leaders is that while young Winston was shunning the syllabus, he was soaking up history, mastering English, reading for pleasure, and learning poetry. He debated history and the essay techniques of Stephenson, Thomas Huxley, and others with his army class master. At fourteen, he dictated English essays for an older boy who in exchange, did Winston's Latin prep.

Many a top executive has left school for more authentic experiences in life or business and, like Churchill, found true learning outside the prescribed boundaries. Though Churchill was clearly gifted, he had also, through his own inclinations, acquired a firm foundation of knowledge. No matter the age or experience of an executive or manager, everyone benefits from a solid grounding in the fundamentals by reading authors of substance and style.

SELF-DIRECTION

The other key to Churchill's ability to speak and write was that he designed and completed his own virtual Dale Carnegie courses. Future leaders do not depend on others for their education. As a twenty-one-year-old subaltern in British India, Churchill filled the sweltering afternoons with work. While others were resting he was reading. He devoured the eight volumes of Gibbon's *Decline and Fall of the Roman Empire*. He juggled several books "at a time to avoid tedium." His breadth was extraordinary by any standards. It ranged, for example, from Aristotle to Laing's *Modern Science and Modern Thought*

HIS OWN UNIVERSITY

Churchill never stopped learning. He studied history, politics, the military, and top thinkers throughout his life. This is his reading list at the age of twenty-one in India.

Annual Register (twenty-seven volumes)

Darwin, *On the Origin of Species*

Henry Fawcett, *Manual of Political Economy*

Edward Gibbon, *The Decline and Fall of the Roman Empire* (eight volumes), *Memoirs of My Life and Writings*

Hallam, *Constitutional History*

Laing, *Modern Science and Modern Thought*

Thomas Macaulay, *History of England* (four volumes), *Essays* (two volumes)

Malthus, *An Essay on the Principle of Population*

Plato, *The Republic*

Winwood Reade, *The Martyrdom of Man*

Schopenhauer, *The Pessimist's Handbook*

Adam Smith, *Wealth of Nations* (two volumes)

and Adam Smith. Like many a modern businessman or politician his reading was remarkably practical.

The ambitious Churchill set out to absorb the parliamentary history of the nineteenth century in the *Annual Registry*, a staggering hundred volumes of debates and party battles. He set down his thoughts on the issues covered in twenty-seven volumes (all his mother could afford). He was essentially reviewing case studies, much as an MBA might do at business school or as an executive reads accounts of companies in the *Harvard Business Review*. "Of course the *Annual Register* is valuable only for its facts," Churchill wrote. "A good knowledge of these would arm me with a sharp sword. Macaulay, Gibbon, Plato, etc must train the muscles to wield that sword to the greatest effect."

Leaders often rise through bursts of self-directed learning. Extracurricular study is just as advisable today for the modern corporate executive or budding leader. Success is about far more than mastering your field on your own terms. Whatever your business or occupation, rich experience and a robust education are the surest course to the development of a true and unique voice.

Becoming a strong speaker, however, is not something to be learned from a book. Leaders need role models. Interestingly, Churchill has attributed much of his ability as an orator not to any number of Englishmen, but to a dynamic American politician he met in New York on his way to Cuba in 1895. Bourke Cochran was a charismatic Tammany Hall Democrat who combined the merits of a strong argument with a rich style. Aged forty-one, he was an admirer of Lady Randolph, having met her two months previously in Paris. A successful lawyer and member of Congress since 1891, he espoused some of the political causes, in particular free trade, that Churchill would take up on entering Parliament. And, like Churchill, he caused considerable controversy by putting his principles before his party and campaigning for the Republican presidential nominee, McKinley, who would become president four years later. Cochran was the first person to recognize Churchill's potential, advising him to study political economy. The two men struck an instant rapport and corresponded regularly until Cochran's death in

1923. "He was my model," wrote Churchill. "I learned from him how to hold thousands in thrall."

A couple of years later Churchill wrote an article entitled "The Scaffolding of Rhetoric," outlining his early ideas on oratory. His central tenet was simple and applies to nearly all forms of business as well as political communications: Find the strongest reason in an argument and marshal all the available facts behind it. Churchill developed rapidly as a speaker partly because he recognized the critical role that oratory would play in his growth as a political leader.

Churchill's self-directed learning and war-crossed life gave him a vitality and freshness that reverberated in his speeches, books, and articles. Indeed, Churchill's lifelong friend Violet Asquith later wrote that Churchill's slim formal education and vigorous life, in contrast to, say, the hallowed halls of Eton, "gave him a directness and lack of pretentiousness that his peers too often lacked. "To Winston Churchill," she wrote, "everything under the sun was new, seen and appraised as on the first day of Creation." Churchill feared neither earthy straight talk nor the grand turn. "There was nothing false, inflated or artificial in his eloquence: It was his natural idiom."

SHAPE YOUR STORY

Leaders define themselves by their speeches and writing. Young Winston saw his pen as a way to make a name for himself and open political doors. Churchill's first journalistic dispatches and early books were remarkable for their candor. Churchill vigorously pointed out the faults of the Empire, the bungling of a military campaign, even the warts of a highly regarded general. Churchill's fierce opinions won him critics at home, but he had a pithy, biting answer. He was there and the old rules did not apply: "It is fashionable in English politics to discredit the opinion of people on the spot," he wrote. "They are supposed to be excited and prejudiced, to be unable to take the judicial and comprehensive views which can, it is believed, be adopted only in an atmosphere of ignorant indifference."

Churchill was a master at shaping each article, book, speech, letter, or memo to fulfill specific purposes. Although he wrote critically acclaimed biographies of his father, Lord Randolph, and ancestor the Duke of Marlborough, most of his writing was about events in which he played an active part. His history of World War I, for instance, *The World Crisis*, showed his tremendous breadth and reach.

Though writing books and articles was Churchill's principal means of financial support, it was also part of his continuing self-education. Churchill's books supplied him with historical refreshment. One of the most valuable lessons to be drawn from them is that, ironically, they may have helped him live and work more vitally in the present. Reflection is essential for everyone, especially those who reach a position of authority. Churchill's evenings and spare moments were often spent analyzing past battles and policies. Writing *Marlborough* was in itself a political and military lesson. *The World Crisis* gave Churchill a chance to study the tremendous forces at play in the Great War and its aftermath that would lead to the Second World War. Six volumes, encompassing a million words, the history covered the First World War with an immediacy that historians have called timeless. "With what feelings does one lay down Mr Churchill's two-thousandth page," wrote John Maynard Keynes in the *Nation and Athenaeum*. "Gratitude to one who can write with so much eloquence and feeling of things which are part of the lives of all of us of the war generation, but which he saw and knew much closer and clearer. Admiration for his energies of mind and his intense absorption of intellectual interest and elemental emotion on what is for the moment the matter in hand."

Churchill's literary masterpieces demonstrated his knowledge of world affairs but even his lighter works served distinct purposes. Churchill plainly enjoyed writing, and one of his shortest books, *My Early Life*, reads as if it wrote itself and continues to be one of his most popular works. But there was a serious side to Churchill's romantic account of his swashbuckling youth. *My Early Life* was written on the heels of Churchill's loss of office in 1929. The light volume was a straightforward way to maintain a positive public profile at the onset of what would become his years in the wilderness.

Although without office, Churchill remained engaged in political debate throughout the 1930s by means of his trenchant journalism. His articles, especially those warning of the Nazi threat, were a powerful influence. He said that his writing had a "combination of the styles of Macaulay and Gibbon, the staccato antitheses of the former and the rolling sentences and genitival endings of the latter." But Churchill did more than mix soaring passages with straightforward language. He never forgot the fundamentals. A modern leader would do well to study his words on the subject whether commencing a speech, a report, or lengthy memorandum:

> I began to see that writing, especially narrative, was not only an affair of sentences, but of paragraphs. Indeed I thought the paragraph no less important than the sentence. . . . Just as the sentence

contains one idea in all its fullness, so the paragraph should embrace a distinct episode; and as sentences should follow one another in harmonious sequence, so the paragraphs must fit on to one another like the automatic couplings of railway carriages. . . .

PERFORMANCE

Rising above personal challenges is often part of becoming a great speaker. Churchill had to overcome a speech impediment that might have silenced many prospective public speakers. At the age of twenty-one he became so anxious about his problem that he consulted an eminent throat specialist, asking for his speech impediment to be cured. He explained that although he was going into the army, he intended to enter politics and become a minister and could not be haunted with the worry of avoiding words starting an *s*. The doctor found no physical defect and prescribed "practice and perseverance" to cure the disability. Churchill spent countless hours trying to get his tongue around sentences featuring the dreaded letter *s*. He was to be heard walking up and down pronouncing phrases such as "The Spanish ships. I cannot see for they are not in sight." Fortunately, he did not entirely succeed and the defect became his oral signature, helping to give an authentic and instantly recognizable ring to his radio broadcasts.

From the start Churchill learned that most speeches can benefit from controversy or attention. He wanted to make waves, to institute change, to alter opinions. His first public speech was during his final term at the military academy Sandhurst and was a spirited attack on the Purity Campaign of a

Mrs. Ormiston Chant, a prudish woman diligently trying to close a number of raucous music hall bars. His first reported speech came soon after. On home leave from India, he leaped at the opportunity to speak at a Conservative political function at Bath. Churchill took no chances that a speech in the provinces would go unnoticed, sending copies in advance to the London press, an almost unheard of practice in those days.

The speech had many of the hallmarks of Churchill's great speeches later in life. It attacked the brain before it tugged at the heartstrings. Persuasion came before the peroration, which reads like vintage Churchill: "They were not wanting, those who said that in this Jubilee year our Empire has reached the height of its glory and power and that now we shall decline, as Babylon, Carthage and Rome had declined. Do not believe these croakers but give the lie to their dismal croaking by showing that the vigor and vitalilty of our race is unimpaired and that our determination is to uphold the Empire that we have inherited from our fathers as Englishmen, that our flag shall fly high on the sea."

Leaders make their own way, and Churchill was wise to speak and promote his fledgling effort. His speech attracted the attention of the *Daily Mail*, which interviewed him for a series on future leaders, writing presciently that he had qualities that "might make him, almost at will, a great popular leader, a great journalist, or the founder of a great advertising business."

Churchill memorized that speech. He had worked diligently for years at improving his memory, and it became a huge asset. As a boy Churchill honed his power of recollection like a young pianist working the scales. In his first term at Harrow he won a prize open to the entire school by reciting 1,200 lines of Thomas Macaulay without a single mistake. By studying verse, he developed a feeling for rhythm and rhyme.

Churchill's prodigious memory gave him a tremendous advantage in delivering long speeches to Parliament. He would prepare in the days before a big parliamentary speech, practicing quips or parries against any number of possible interjections. Churchill practiced so thoroughly that he seemed to be speaking extemporaneously. Elizabeth Layton, one of his secretaries, recalled his gestures and how "sometimes he would hold the front of his black coat, fingers tucked in, sometimes his hands would be clasped in front of him, sometimes a forefinger would be uplifted. He held his audience (me included) spellbound."

Churchill's slips of the tongue were planned carefully in advance. In his acceptance speech on receiving an honorary degree from Harvard, Churchill seemed to accidentally say "the infernal combustion engine" then quickly corrected it to "the internal combustion engine." The seeming Freudian slip caused considerable amusement. However, Elizabeth Layton had heard him rehearsing the slip while on the train from Washington.

The lesson is simple but requires lots of hard work. Practice is essential, particularly if you want to sound spontaneous.

One slip Churchill did not plan came early in his career. During a lengthy parliamentary speech in favor of free trade his mind went blank in the midst of a sentence. To a lesser man it might have been devastating: two aborted attempts to pick up where he left off ended in vain. He sat down clumsily, mumbling and apologizing. CHURCHILL BREAKS DOWN, DRAMATIC SCENE IN THE HOUSE OF COMMONS read a newspaper headline the next day.

But Churchill was not down for long. He had simply lost his train of thought after speaking for nearly three-quarters of an hour. His memory was fine, but wisely he decided he was not going to take another chance. Henceforth, his speeches were generally written out in advance, and he had the text in hand, a wise practice for even the most competent executive.

Excerpt from Churchill's Famous "Never in the Field of Human Conflict" Speech

Never in the field of human conflict was so much owed by so many to so few.

All hearts go out to the Fighter pilots, whose brilliant actions we see with our own eyes day after day,

but we must never forget that all the time,

night after night, month after month,

our Bomber Squadrons travel far into Germany, find their targets in the darkness by the highest navigational skill, aim their attacks, often under the heaviest fire often at serious loss,

with deliberate careful precision, and inflict shattering blows upon the whole of the technical and war-making structure of the Nazi power.

TUNING IN TO THE AUDIENCE

In 1904 an election was in the air. The government was for protection of trade. Churchill was for free trade. A few words at a public meeting illustrate how perfectly he was tuned in to his audience. He avoided confronting them with detailed arguments. He nailed the government as protectionists and, in a short inventory of their policies, hammered the message home. He also had a keen sense of the average listener's attention span, delivering his message in the first few opening words, while the audience was alert. The clinching argument, which people would have taken away with them, came in the last ten words.

The great leader of the protectionist party, whatever else you may or may not think about him, has at any rate left me in no doubt as to what use he will make of his victory if he should win it. We know perfectly what to expect—a party of great vested interests, banded together in a formidable confederation, corruption at home, aggression to cover it up abroad, the trickery of tariff juggles, the tyranny of a party machine; sentiment by the bucketful, patriotism by the imperial pint, the open hand at the public exchequer, the open hand at the public house, dear food for the million, cheap labour for the millionaire.

Many modern politicians and businessmen would love to dish out such artful sound bites. Those were the days when people turned up in hundreds and thousands to public meetings. They were attuned to political thought and would have appreciated and understood such phrases as "sentiment by the bucketful, patriotism by the imperial pint," recognizing the government's ploy of shrugging off the protectionist label by allowing imperial preference for goods from the Empire.

TIMING

As Churchill developed his formidable wit and verbal arsenal, he continued to prepare his parliamentary set pieces. He perfected his timing, which, aided by his spontaneous wit, could unnerve the butt of his humor.

Typical was the occasion when a speaker, seeing Churchill shaking his head, interrupted his prepared statement to say, "I see the Right Hon Gentleman shaking his head. I wish to remind him that I am only stating my own opinion." Churchill's deadpan reply was devastating. "And I am only shaking my own head."

Churchill could also sting by appearing to be bored, just as an executive in a meeting can catch someone out by not appearing to be listening. Sometimes during an opposition speech his eyelids would grow heavy and he would appear to be slumbering. "Must you fall asleep when I am speaking?" demanded a petulant member of Parliament. "No," came the reply, to general amusement. "It is purely voluntary."

TEAM CHURCHILL

Executives and managers can learn much from Churchill's team approach to accomplishing colossal amounts of work.

He understood the importance of targeted research. As a young man, he wrote dozens of letters to generals and others, asking for their memories and opinions on events as he completed the narratives of his first books. Early success in writing and speaking permitted him the convenience of hiring a secretary in 1901 when he was just twenty-seven. At first Churchill dictated to ease the burden of his voluminous correspondence. But the young parliamentarian soon began dictating everything—speeches, articles, and books.

Just as an executive needs contributions from managers and assistants when compiling lengthy reports or speeches, Churchill quickly mastered the art of marshaling talent. He excelled at tackling big projects. He hired the best researchers, often young Oxford graduates, and consulted with a variety of specialists. Assistants might produce some ten thousand words on a specific historical period to give Churchill enough information to begin dictating. If he began a chapter while his knowledge was still incomplete, his further inquiries would fill in the gaps.

Many an executive or manager can learn from Churchill's method. Speeches, reports, and other communications can often be started when only the skeletal facts are known. The best innovators push ahead before they know all the answers. Indeed it is often the means of discovering what you need to know.

Churchill was not perfect. He would grow impatient. When he did, he invariably apologized later; "Good heavens," he said once to a secretary he thought was upset. "You musn't mind me. We're all toads beneath the harrow, you know." It was the means of getting things done.

Writer's block was no worry to Churchill. Dictation permitted him to accomplish a tremendous amount of work. Today, with the latest advances in digital dictation, it is a skill that all sorts of managers and executives should master. Churchill's most productive hours of dictation were often at night, and he was known to dictate from both bed and bath. He might start by digesting a paper written by an assistant or review a few letters responding to his queries. The first of a relay team of secretaries stood at the ready. The actual act of creation became a performance, with Churchill pacing and gesturing as his secretary waited on every word.

He would pause on a word or phrase, feeling for the right meaning before hitting his stride. "He carefully savoured and chose his words," said his Private Secretary Sir John Martin, "often testing alternative words or phrases in a low mutter before coming out loudly with the final choice." Interruptions by secretaries, assistants, or friends were frowned upon. Churchill's eccentric method turned what to others might seem an endless daily grind of producing thousands of words into entertainment. Wherever he dictated, and that could literally be anywhere, at least one secretary was listening. The fact that someone else was always involved helped Churchill maintain his amazing productivity.

FINDING YOUR VOICE

Critics have mistakenly viewed Churchill's technique as "writing by committee." It is true that Churchill did employ a team of assistants to help with his histories but the crux is what he did with their material. The actual final act of creation was distinctly Churchillian, a model for modern-day leaders. "I might have given him some memorandum before dinner, four or five hours before," recalled one of his researchers, Bill Deakin. "Now he would walk up and down dictating. My facts were there, but he had seen it in a deeper perspective. My memorandum was only a frame; it ignited his imagination."

The infusion of expert and routine assistance, everything from Oxford researchers to the teams of secretaries, turned what might have become a dreary grind into a buzzing industry.

Elizabeth Layton, one of Churchill's secretaries, told of a typical speech-writing session. In 1943, the young secretary found herself with Churchill at the White House. "He had been dining with the President and around midnight came to his own quarters saying that there was a busy night ahead. He was about to dictate his speech to Congress. With pencils and notebook, I settled into a high-backed chair in his room. He began pacing about. Inspiration came and he began dictating, voice rising and falling, hands gesturing as if making the actual speech. While pacing behind my chair he tore off his dinner jacket. The next time his waistcoat came off. The third time there was a longer pause and a rustling noise as something flew through the air on to the bed. When he again came into view he was wearing his famous green and gold dragon dressing gown. At two-thirty he finished. At four-thirty I had typed it out. As I tottered off to bed an American duty officer said, "Gee are you crazy. All the American girls went home twelve hours ago."

There was no set pattern. Sometimes Elizabeth would follow him around the garden taking shorthand. On one occasion he began to dictate a broadcast from his bed less than two hours before he was due on air; the script was thrust into his hands as he approached the microphone.

When composing a speech, Churchill instructed that the typewritten draft be typed in psalm style, to help him with the rhythm and pace. Abbreviations saved space and helped with the phrasing, as in this brief excerpt from his speech to the Allied governments, December 6, 1941:

In the 22nd month of the war
    against Nazism,
    we meet here in this old palace
            of St. James's,
    itself not unscarred
        by the fire of the enemy,
    to proclaim the high purposes and resolves
        of the lawful constitutional
            Govts. of Europe
            Whose countries hv bn overrun, . . .

He edited proofs while sitting in bed or standing at his sloping desk. "Until I see the existing material in type I cannot make progress."

Churchill proved that a tremendously busy statesman can produce an immense amount of high-quality work—Nobel Prize–winning books and some of history's most stirring speeches—while maintaining a distinct and original voice. Churchill showed how to benefit from all the advantages of a team approach to research and preparation without falling into a trap which ensnares some executives: producing speeches that sound as if they were written by committee.

Churchill recognized that his huge workload made professional assistance critical. On his books, especially, he gained by having a skilled eye view the finished product. Note the points he makes in a letter to his long-serving private secretary, Edward Marsh, concerning the proofs of *Marlborough*. More than a few executives would benefit by giving a similar checklist to a talented assistant. Churchill asked Marsh to be on the lookout for faulty grammar, awkward or "dull" phrases, "vulgar" or "cheap references," and adjectives he tended to overuse.

Churchill was often "delighted" at the way Marsh had "increased in some instances the precision, in others the euphony, of a sentence." The lesson for today's leaders is that if a supremely talented communicator such as Winston Churchill benefited from having others help research and review his work you, too, might get assistance in preparing and fine-tuning a report or speech.

The Churchill method has the advantage of being both practical and highly creative. Dictate or write from this solid foundation, and you'll find you can dramatically reduce the time necessary to create a communication while maintaining your own distinct and individual voice.

CHURCHILLIAN PRINCIPLES

- Strike when the voice or pen is hot.
- Marshal teams to tackle big speeches or reports.
- Tune in to the audience.
- Always demand something of your audience.
- Remember the fundamentals. Read broadly to obtain a sense of history, and read classic books of substance and style.
- Study and rehearse to become an accomplished public speaker.
- Develop a sense of timing. Master the pause.
- Make the speech or report your own by stamping it indelibly with your own voice.

CHAPTER 4

Be Magnanimous

I was once asked to devise an inscription for a monument in France. I wrote "In War, Resolution. In Defeat, Defiance. In Victory, Magnanimity. In Peace, Goodwill."

—Winston Churchill, *My Early Life*, 1930

———

Churchill won the devotion and dedication of countless men and women in Britain and throughout the free world during World War II. The Churchill faithful at home ranged from the eclectic network of informants that sprang up to aid his intelligence efforts in the 1930s to the broad coalition he led during the war. They were Liberals, Socialists, and Conservatives, former foes and longtime allies. A lesser man might have harbored grudges and shunned many of these talented men who had opposed him in the past, but the strongest leaders are magnanimous and believe in the power of forgiveness.

In the epic struggle against Hitler and Nazi Germany, Churchill had no time for petty grievances or old scores. He needed to enlist every capable man and woman in Britain's fight for survival. Churchill's long career in diverse government posts both as a Conservative and a Liberal gave him a flexibility of mind and a deeper understanding of human nature than his lesser colleagues. Warren Bennis, in his book *On Becoming a Leader*, speaks of this essential journey as "the process of becoming an integrated human being." Churchill epitomized this process. Confident leaders see no conflict in being both tough and fair. Thus as a soldier he had, with few qualms, shot men in close combat, but as a Liberal parliamentarian he was an advocate for basic rights and social justice. A decade or so after fighting in South Africa's Boer War, Churchill, as Home Secretary, pushed through major reforms to the British criminal justice system. He believed in the power of giving second chances, especially to those who had made mistakes. Throughout his career Churchill reached out to those who for one reason or another had been on opposite sides of major debates. He was a strikebreaker one day and a peacemaker another, with a rare ability to set personal feelings to one side during the resolution of major conflicts. As he famously told Harry Hopkins, Roosevelt's personal assistant, he hated no one and did not feel he had any enemies except the Huns, and that was a professional issue.

Churchill demonstrated that the most resolute leaders can also be the most forgiving and resourceful. Consider the situation Churchill faced in June 1940, just five weeks after becoming prime minister. The war was going badly, morale was low. Parliament was falling into a game of second-guessing the government's strategies. No one would have been more justified than Churchill in reminding Parliament how the previous ministers had failed to take his advice to rearm before the war and to act more decisively during its early months. But Churchill knew that recrimination would not be in the interests of the nation. The last thing he wanted was publicly to assign blame. He thought it foolish in the extreme to indict those responsible for the perilous situation in which the country had been placed. Without evading the facts of earlier disastrous judgments, he declared that the guilty were "too many." He suggested that each man search his conscience. Then, even though he was blameless, he added "I frequently search mine." Churchill knew that a witch-hunt would divert attention from more important matters. "Of this I am certain," he warned, "that if we open a quarrel between the past and the present, we shall find that we have lost the future."

Churchill's philosophy paralleled Lincoln's classic foreboding of the Civil War, "A house divided against itself cannot stand." Churchill was setting a tone of unity for his administration, getting on with business, telling both his own people and his enemies that henceforth Britain was united. Business leaders must do this all the time with staff, partners, and enemies, even if it does not always come easily. Steve Jobs, for instance, was celebrated more for his vision and temper than his management skills in founding Apple Computer. But when Jobs rejoined the faltering company as president in 1997, he surprised the Apple faithful by launching a strategic alliance with the company's longtime nemesis, Bill Gates. Many within Apple had wanted Jobs to continue pursuing the company's lawsuit against Microsoft. Instead, Jobs settled the dispute with Microsoft and garnered a $150 million stock investment in Apple. He was burying old wounds, moving on. Wall Street cheered the news and Apple began another of its legendary comebacks.

WEARING MAGNANIMITY

Magnanimity does not come easily. Leaders do not pick it up like a season's fashion. A man or woman blessed with magnanimity wears it through and through. Magnanimity can be an immensely powerful factor in leadership but it should not be confused with, or led astray by, loyalty. Churchill was a man with intense personal feelings and he occasionally fell victim to a weakness shared by many great leaders. He not only forgave but kept in power men he should have simply sacked, such as Admiral Fisher, the erratic genius whose ambivalence over the Dardanelles campaign caused Churchill so much anguish during World War I.

In his book *Leadership,* James MacGregor Burns writes of the transforming power of leadership in raising "the level of human conduct and ethical aspiration of both leader and led." Sometimes simply getting people to let go of the past can transform an organization. Churchill did this both with individuals and on a national scale. For example, before World War II, Colin Thorton-Kemsley, an active member in Churchill's parliamentary constituency, had been one of his harshest critics. He had also worked to keep Churchill out of office. But war changed his mind. The former opponent wrote to Churchill that the statesman's warnings about the "German danger" had been right and that he was not proud of his past opposition. He asked for no reply, but Churchill was not one to let old grievances fester. A man confessing his errors is a man asking to join your cause. He wrote: "I certainly think that Englishmen ought to start fair with one another from the outset in so grievous a struggle, and as far as I am concerned the past is dead."

REVENGE IS SWEET BUT EXPENSIVE

The weight on Churchill's shoulders, combined with his high expectations for those around him, could at times make him irascible and moody. But in things large and small, Churchill's essential humanity carried him through. Like Lincoln's, his compassionate nature was an advantage in times of conflict.

CHURCHILL CALLING FOR MAGNANIMITY

The tide of war has at last turned in our favour. I urge generous counsels upon the people of Natal. Many eyes are upon
you now, all admiring, some reluctantly admiring. Let not
these watching multitudes be surprised and disappointed.
Do not act or speak so it may be said, "it is true the Natal
colonists have fought well; but they were drunk with racial
animosity. They were brave in battle; but they are spiteful in
victory." (Excerpt from an article for the *South African Natal Witness,*
March 29, 1900)

Clement Attlee, a Socialist who, before serving as Churchill's
deputy in the wartime coalition government, had often opposed him in Parliament, considered compassion to be his
greatest virtue. Churchill not only sympathized with the pain
of others: he acted. Moved to tears after visiting a town that had
been devastated by German bombs, Churchill declared that
the government had to do "something about that damage
now." Within a day officials launched the War Damage Commission to effect speedy compensation.

Leaders become compassionate by responding quickly and
humanely to hardship and suffering. There is no shortcut.
Churchill's early military experiences shaped his philosophy
of magnanimity. After riding in Britain's last cavalry charge in
Omdurman, Churchill paid tribute to the thousands of massa-
cred Dervishes, "Yet these were as brave men as ever walked the
earth." In South Africa, after the Boers had been driven from

Natal, the smell of victory inspired a call for vengeance. British South Africans and the London establishment clamored for punishment of the rebels, especially the British-born naturalized burghers who had sided with the Boers. Although riding a wave of international acclaim after his dramatic escape from a Boer prison, Churchill did not allow his ambition to curb his criticism of the popular view. In a telegram to the London *Morning Post* and in a letter published in the *Natal Witness* he preached a policy of magnanimity, writing, "Revenge may be sweet but it is also most expensive." What is especially interesting to modern leaders is that the young Churchill recognized how hard it would be to persuade people on purely moral grounds. Churchill couched his plea for reconciliation, "the fusion and concord of the Dutch and British races," in a pragmatic vein. "An eye for an eye and a tooth for a tooth," he wrote, were not worth "five years of bloody partisan warfare and the consequent impoverishment of South Africa."

But British casualties were mounting and there was little stomach for magnanimity toward the Boers. The *Morning Post* printed Churchill's conciliatory letter but ran an editorial demanding the enemy be punished. Churchill was unmoved. On entering Parliament, he continued to urge conciliation and became a close friend of the Boer commander, General Louis Botha. So it is that one of Churchill's earliest calls for magnanimity offers another valuable lesson. To urge reconciliation among bitter foes is neither popular nor easy. Like so much of true leadership it requires independent thought and courage.

The next time you feel an urge for revenge, consider the lightly traveled path of magnanimity and reconciliation. Not only will you rest easier. It will probably be good for business.

BREAK BREAD

As Churchill grew into his role as a statesman and leader, he excelled at winning over opponents in seemingly intractable disputes. Fortunately it was in his nature. Many of his government posts required Churchill to resolve management disputes or orchestrate diplomatic solutions. Often he had to set aside bruised feelings before he could negotiate a solution. Such was the situation he faced late in World War I. As Minister of Munitions, Churchill had pledged to produce "masses of guns, mountains of shells, clouds of aeroplanes." But by the time he arrived in the job, union leaders at key munitions factories had threatened production with a series of destabilizing strikes. They had also been arrested and forbidden to return to the factories. Three consecutive ministers of munitions had balked at the demands of the union leaders to be reinstated, and the head of the giant forge in Glasgow, Sir William Beardmore, refused any talk of compromise.

Churchill, however, recognized immediately that he could not realize his promise of increased munitions without the full support of the labor leaders. Two weeks into his new position as Minister of Munitions, he telegraphed his chief labor adviser, Sir Thomas Munro, asking him to try to soften the opposition and encourage the company to rise above questions of what he called sentiment or principle. "Please go and see Sir William Beardmore and explain to him that I think it would be better to take these men back as a matter of course without raising any question of sentiment or principle on so small a point. If they do not really want reinstatement but only a political grievance this will soon become apparent in their daily work. If Sir William does not share my view I hope he will at once come to see me as trouble may easily be fomented on this point." Churchill was advocating a calm and practical approach even though the suggestion of hiring back the union leaders might have risked precipitating a new crisis.

When Munro reported that Beardmore was unmoved, Churchill seemed destined to become the fourth minister unable to resolve the crisis. But Churchill took the bull by the horns. He invited the leader of the exiled workers, David Kirkwood, to the Ministry, an approach his predecessors had apparently not considered. Though Kirkwood expected him to be arrogant and abrupt, Churchill greeted him simply, disarming him with a complete lack of pretension. A surprisingly friendly Churchill set the labor leader at ease. Kirkwood was told that he was essential to the war effort and that, whatever their differences, nothing was to be allowed "to stand in the way of the production of the munitions of war."

Kirkwood agreed, whereupon Churchill rang a bell, announcing, "Let's have a cup of tea and a bit of cake together." This simple gesture made a huge impression on Kirkwood. They had resolved nothing except the important understanding that they shared the same ultimate goal. But by offering tea and cakes, what Kirkwood called "the bread and salt of friendship," the two could speak frankly about their differences and with less rancor. Kirkwood threatened to interrupt the operations of countless factories if he was not taken back. Churchill declared that he would not stand for such talk in the Ministry of Munitions, but Kirkwood replied that he would talk that way in the "Court of Heaven" and not only say it but "do it." That inspired a fiery Churchillian stare, a roar of laughter, and the admission, "By Jove, and I believe you would." While acknowledging that Kirkwood felt wronged, Churchill said there was no point in "getting heated about it," and said he would see what he could do. Three days later Kirkwood was hired as manager at the Beardmore Mile-End Shell Factory. He instituted a bonus scheme that within six weeks had the factory leading the nation in shell production.

By meeting and breaking bread with an opponent, Churchill looked beyond the anger of past disputes to reach an agreement that earned the commitment of thousands of workers. That apt lesson in leadership was even more impressive because it was accomplished in an age when owners feared their factories would be crippled by the spread of Bolshevism. Churchill's conservative critics decried his offer of the "hand of fellowship" to "desperate agitators." They could hardly have been more wrong. Churchill's hand, cake, and forgiveness produced the shells Britain needed to win the war.

FRIENDSHIP OVER BLOOD

When a crisis demanded it, Churchill answered force with force. But he was also among the first to urge conciliation and compromise. There is much to learn from how he approached the seemingly intractable problem of Irish home rule, and the legendary Michael Collins. In 1919 the British had put a price of five thousand pounds on the head of the charismatic IRA leader. The offer of a reward accomplished little. Eighteen Englishmen were murdered that year. In early 1920 the violence spread and Sinn Féin drew up a short list of targets for assassination, including the Prime Minister and Winston Churchill. Responding in kind, Churchill, as Secretary of State for War, established a "Special Emergency Gendarme," known as the Black and Tans, to combat terrorism.

When they became guilty of many of the same excesses as the IRA, Churchill urged that the Black and Tans be disciplined and reined in. Less than six months later, he threw his support behind the offer of a truce. He persuaded the cabinet of the importance of reaching a settlement. Britain had already played rough. Now, Churchill argued, was the time to lower the guns and resolve their differences.

Churchill's words in cabinet are just as relevant today to leaders intent on resolving disputes: "If you are strong enough you should make the effort. Where is the disadvantage? There is no military disadvantage. . . . the truce will be kept or it will be broken. If kept you'll have a tremendous advantage; they'll have a great difficulty in getting men to go back."

Within months a truce was struck and a conference called to negotiate the future of Ireland. In October of 1921 when Michael Collins and Arthur Griffith, president of Sinn Féin, arrived at Number 10 Downing Street to meet the Cabinet, most of the ministers saw Collins and Griffith as murderers. Churchill, however, saw them rather differently and, always adept at getting along with erstwhile adversaries, took Collins home. Leaders have a knack for seeing the best in their opponents, for admiring their strengths even as they question their positions.

Churchill had a gift for breaking the ice one to one, for bridging the gap between himself and an opponent by securing some common point of reference. Humor and timing were his weapons. Churchill amused Collins, making him eat his own words, surprising him by quoting a biting, skeptical analysis the IRA leader had written of Churchill: "Will sacrifice all for political gain . . . Inclined to be bombastic . . . Don't actually trust him." At one point Collins made an angry, per-

sonal charge. "You hunted me day and night!" he exclaimed.
"You put a price on my head!" As Churchill described in his
memoirs he had a ready rejoinder: "'Wait a minute', I said.
'You are not the only one'. And I took from my wall the framed
copy of the reward offered for my recapture by the Boers. 'At
any rate it was a good price, £5,000. Look at me, £25 dead or
alive. How would you like that?'"

Churchill lost none of his toughness during each day's formal negotiations. He demanded Britain have the "free use of
the Irish coasts in peace or war." And when a Sinn Féin memorandum countered that Dublin must control naval defense,
Churchill made it clear that this was in no way acceptable.
"This able memorandum will shorten the task of this committee, in fact will bring it to an end," he declared. "It amounts to
a reasoned, measured, uncompromising refusal to meet us at
any point."

Churchill moved the talks forward by winning Collins's
trust. The treaty was signed on December 6, 1921, but there remained the issue of what to do with the Sinn Féin members
awaiting the death penalty for murder. Churchill realized the
issue would cause further problems for Collins in Dublin and
wisely and compassionately, he made certain that the IRA prisoners and leaders were "informed privately that the extreme
sentence will not be carried out."

What can prospective leaders learn from Churchill's role in
the tense negotiations over Irish home rule? Churchill managed to befriend and earn the trust of the leader of a group
originally set on murdering him. Never abandoning his basic
position, Churchill let anger and resentment recede and deployed his humor and charm to win a successful agreement.

The next time you face a competitor or enemy, consider

how you might use magnanimity to your advantage. Compassionate leaders have the foresight and good sense to achieve a successful compromise with even the most bitter foe.

CHURCHILLIAN PRINCIPLES

- Magnanimity breeds trust and loyalty among subordinates and partners.
- Seeking revenge harms the victor as well as the vanquished.
- Break bread with opponents to sidestep anger and reach understanding.
- Be magnanimous toward those who lack your ability or good fortune and you will find that former opponents become friends and allies.
- Urge conciliation and compromise when personal animosities and differences of opinion threaten the resolution of a crisis.

CHAPTER 5

Resist Bullies

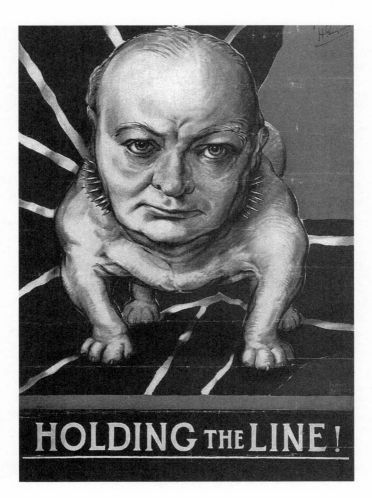

If you should be thrown into a quarrel, you should bear yourself so that an opponent may be aware of it. . . . Pugnacity and will power cannot be dispensed with.

—Winston Churchill, Parliament, January 31, 1947

———

Churchill was a master at dealing with bullies of any sort, from the green benches of Parliament to the Kremlin. His extraordinary will and strength of character were tremendous assets against his foes, but equally important was his readiness to tackle the unpredictable. Since Churchill assumed he couldn't be certain of a bully's next move, he was prepared for a range of possibilities.

He had an instinctive understanding of the innate chaos that underlies conflict, a phenomenon Tom Peters explored in his book *Thriving on Chaos.* "Predictability is a thing of the past," wrote Peters. "We have no idea" who will be our partners "next week, let alone next month." Peters might well have been writing about Churchill in the 1930s. The statesman mastered a central prewar paradox that so many other world leaders failed to untangle: to ensure peace, Britain had to rearm, while to negotiate with Hitler, tempting as it seemed to many at the time, would only make war inevitable. When the Cold War broke out in a war-weary Western world in the late forties, and a former ally became an implacable enemy, his message to Parliament on December 14, 1950, had echoes of the thirties; it was necessary to remain strong: "Appeasement from strength is magnanimous and noble, and might be the surest and perhaps the only path to peace."

STUDY YOUR BULLY

Bullies are a fact of life and business. At some point nearly every business faces a bigger, stronger competitor. The best organizations seem to revel in the chance to show their mettle against a skilled competitor. In *Good to Great*, Jim Collins writes that a company's response to a threat is a strong indicator of its long-term prospects. Those who tremble at being matched against top competitors often perform weakly. But "great" companies seem to rise to the occasion. They feel "exhilarated by the idea of going up against the best."

Churchill loved nothing better than a worthy adversary. Equally important, he saw them coming. He had an uncanny ability to divine and confront far-off threats. Today's business leaders must do much the same thing in the marketplace. Companies have to anticipate harassing lawsuits, anticompetitive practices, monopoly pricing, and other forms of commercial bullying. The prepared executive and company are ready to respond with a variety of countermeasures. Those who fail to resist a bully invariably regret it.

Leaders have to stand up to a variety of people in climbing up the ladder, including bosses. The steel titan Andrew Carnegie wrote: "Boss your boss just as soon as you can; try it on early. There is nothing he will like so well if he is the right kind of boss; if he is not, he is not the man for you to remain with, leave him whenever you can, even at a present sacrifice, and find one capable of discerning genius."

Churchill faced the ultimate task. The greatest bully of the twentieth century, Adolf Hitler, at the head of a totalitarian regime armed to the teeth, was threatening the whole of Europe. But Churchill was out of power, written off by many as past his prime. Churchill's long, often solitary, fight during the 1930s, has been dubbed the Wilderness Years. What is remarkable is that during this harsh decade Churchill became the leader who would stand up to the bully by hammering resolve into people who felt threatened by the chaotic situation. His internal gyroscope always sorted out the greatest threats to Britain. He showed extraordinary resilience and flexibility in proposing a series of countermoves against Hitler and German rearmament. Churchill proved that confronting and resisting bullies are critical elements of leadership.

What's the price of not standing up to a bully? In *Execution*, Bossidy and Charan write of a company "so terrified of Microsoft, they were pulling their punches." And Microsoft wasn't even their competitor. Fear of adversaries, real or imagined, will not help get the job done. You've got to overcome your trepidation and look upon the competition as a worthy challenger.

GRAB FIRSTHAND INFORMATION

Much like the best executives, Churchill took command of a problem by first acquiring a wealth of firsthand information. When it came to Hitler and Germany, he began with the Treaty of Versailles, which settled the scale of reparations to be made by Germany at the end of World War I. Despite international clamor for revenge, Churchill argued that the treaty's vindictive and unrealistic conditions would inflame resentment and national pride in Germany. "The soul of Germany smoulders with dreams of a War of Liberation or Revenge," Churchill wrote. Over the years, he called repeatedly for a revision of the treaty in "cold blood."

As Hitler rose in power, Churchill made it a point to read everything he could about him. When he read and analyzed *Mein Kampf,* he became aware that the warlike character of the original had been watered down in translation. Repulsed by the book's blatant anti-Semitism and hatred of all that is free and democratic, Churchill had little doubt that Hitler's objectives and the theme of *Mein Kampf* were one and the same, a racist call to arms to "restore the German nation" and conquer others through war. In the late 1920s this was not as obvious as it is today. World War I had drained Britain and France of their youth and hope. Peace at any cost dominated debates in the parliaments of Britain and France. Anti-Semitism was rampant in Europe, among Britain's ruling class, and in America.

Churchill listened to Hitler's propaganda disavowing aggression. He saw through it. Bullies lie and Churchill knew from *Mein Kampf* that Hitler believed that "the great masses of the people . . . will more easily fall victims to a big lie than to a small one." Churchill had no doubt that "Hitler and his followers would seize the first available opportunity to resort to armed force," and said as much to Prince Otto von Bismark, the Counselor at the London German Embassy in late 1931. That year and the next, Churchill wrote of the growing menace of Hitler and the Nazis. In May of 1932 he gave the first of his many formal warnings of war to Parliament, seven years before the storm broke: "I would say to those who would like to see Germany and France on an equal footing in armaments: Do you wish for war?"

In forming his sense of the Nazi threat, Churchill went far

beyond his perceptive reading of *Mein Kampf* and the Treaty of Versailles. On the surface it would seem unlikely that Churchill could discover so much when he was out of power, lacking the formal mechanisms to learn about his enemy. But the best leaders are sponges for information, especially in a crisis. Through an amazing web of friends and informants, Churchill made himself a magnet to all those who feared Hitler and the consequences of German rearmament. His search for insights and details about Britain's enemy was inspired and exhaustive, foreshadowing the methods of the best modern executives. "Much of my day is spent acquiring information," wrote Andy Grove, the former chairman of Intel. "I read standard reports and memos but also get information ad hoc. I talk to people inside and outside the company, managers at other firms, financial analysts and members of the press."

Speaking in Parliament, Churchill warned of the threat of Hitler early on: "Herr Hitler has torn up the Treaties and garrisoned the Rhineland. His troops are there, and they are going to stay. All this means that the Nazi regime has gained a new prestige in Germany and all the neighbouring countries. I do not doubt that the whole of the German frontier is to be fortified . . . The moment those are completed, the whole aspect of middle Europe is changed."

Churchill sought out businessmen, tourists, refugees, British officers, journalists, and friends or relatives just back from Germany and questioned them on every aspect of the threatening developments in Germany. During the 1930s Churchill met several times with the Soviet ambassador to Britain and picked up tidbits from diplomats in the countries bordering Germany. By calling on industrialists at home and abroad, he gleaned figures on the production of armaments. Churchill created his own intelligence network, what Professor G. Nicholas of Oxford has called "a private information center, the information of which was often superior to that of the government." His skill in cultivating and maintaining these sources is in itself a valuable lesson in leadership. Some of these men, like Major Desmond Morton, Wing Commander Tor Anderson, and Ralph Wigram, held official positions and were jeopardizing their careers by providing what was often secret intelligence. Others were talented private citizens, like Professor Frederick Lindemann, a top physicist and professor of experimental philosophy at Oxford. The results of this information stream were immediate and far reaching, for Churchill turned this loose-knit group of men and women into an informal team secretly working against Hitler and Nazi Germany.

INFORMATION AS A WEAPON

Too many executives think of information as something static that comes to you and requires little sweat or analysis. Churchill's experience as a government minister and journalist taught him to use information as a weapon. He checked and double-checked it until he was confident it could be used reliably against his political opponents.

In order to compete effectively against external enemies, budding leaders often have to first overcome bullies within their own ranks. Before Churchill could defeat Hitler, he had to confront the bullies in the British government who were peddling their policy of appeasement. First Prime Minister Stanley Baldwin, and then his successor, Neville Chamberlain, did all they could to discredit Churchill and undermine his arguments. At times they willfully misled the public and implied that Churchill's comparison of British and German armaments was wrong. Churchill was mocked and, in an allusion to his mother's distant Native American blood, even called a half-breed.

Baldwin and his party whips strove to paint Churchill as an erratic, untrustworthy genius. Churchill stuck to his facts and figures. In 1934, he challenged Baldwin and the government. Churchill had already foreseen that Britain's strength in the air would be critical to her survival. Now he warned the government that falling behind Germany's air force would be tantamount to a "high crime against the state." Baldwin had to respond. He blustered with his usual charge that Churchill's figures were exaggerated and strangely asserted he could not "look further forward than the next two years." Then he made a solemn pledge: "His Majesty's Government are determined in no condition to accept any position of inferiority with regard to what air force may be raised in Germany in the future."

Baldwin had been lured into a trap. Within months Churchill had discredited him, telling Parliament, "It cannot be disputed that both in numbers and in quality Germany has already obtained a marked superiority over our Home Defence Air Force." Cornered, Baldwin was forced to admit he and his government had broken their solemn vow.

Churchill had to overcome a lot more bullying to rally the British people. Just as successful, complacent companies are often not ready to hear that their dominance may be under attack, Britain was simply not ready for the frightening truth that it was woefully unprepared for Hitler. Leaders have to keep fighting a war of information. In 1936 Churchill invited a key government figure for a swim at Chartwell and gleaned a powerful bit of intelligence, the assertion from reliable German refugees that the Germans were spending a billion pounds a year on arms. Churchill set out to see if it was really true. He asked his friend, Sir Henry Strakosch, who headed a company in London, if he could look into it. (Churchill frequently checked his information with all sorts of experts, including heads of foreign states.) Weeks later, after putting the brains of his company on to the question, the executive reported that the figure was certainly accurate.

Armed with this information, Churchill, as he put it, "accosted" Chamberlain, then Chancellor of the Exchequer, in the lobby of the House of Commons and told him he would confront him with the figure the following day in Parliament and ask him to confirm or deny the damning evidence. Chamberlain could not deny it and was forced to admit publicly that he had "no official figures." Thus Churchill had made two irrefutable points: the Germans were furiously rearming and Chamberlain and the government were hopelessly out of touch with a fundamental issue of national security—how much Britain's mortal enemy was spending on arms.

Leaders keep pounding away at bullies, and Churchill stood firm. In late 1937 Chamberlain made the mistake of questioning his judgment in Parliament. Bullies are most vulnerable when they overreach. Churchill recognized Chamberlain had gone too far. He struck back. In a speech to his constituents in Chingford on December 9, he answered Chamberlain's personal taunts with a challenge: "I will gladly submit my judgement about foreign affairs and national defence during the last five years in comparison to his own."

This stirring speech represented a significant victory. Perhaps the most important lesson to be learned from Churchill's battles against Britain's prewar Prime Ministers and Hitler is that when fighting bullies you must often wage a long and arduous campaign. You have to study and make sense out of complex, often chaotic situations. You must enlist the efforts of others toward your goal. And you must be in complete command of your facts.

ATTACK EARLY

Churchill kept a weather eye open for bullies and once they became dangerous, he pushed for immediate action. The key was to stop them before they gained momentum and struck fear in the hearts of their intended victims, what the Nazis dubbed "frightfulness." When the Bolsheviks threatened Poland in the summer of 1920, Churchill wrote, exhorting action, to Bonar Law, a senior Conservative: "All my experience goes to show the advantage of attacking these people. They become very dangerous the moment they think you fear them." Churchill understood, as so many modern leaders do, that bullies use both physical and emotional intimidation. Once bullying goes unchecked, the perpetrators find it much easier the next time. Just as he seldom let a barb in Parliament go unanswered, Churchill felt it a drastic mistake to let a bully strike without retaliation.

In 1918 Bolshevik soldiers murdered the British naval attaché in Petrograd (now Saint Petersburg.) Churchill had no doubt about the correct course of action. He quickly wrote a memo to the War Cabinet, urging the tireless pursuit of the perpetrators of the crime. Note how skillfully Churchill advocated immediate action while laying the groundwork for a more general principle: "The only policy which is likely to be effective, either for the past or the future, is to mark down the personalities of the Bolshevik government as the objects upon whom justice will be executed, however long it takes, and to make them feel that their punishment will become an important object of British policy to be held steadily in view through the phases of the war and of the settlement. . . . The exertions which a nation is prepared to make to protect its individual representatives or citizens from outrage is one of the truest measures of its greatness as an organized state."

If only Jimmy Carter had acted with such strength and determination. When Iranian militants unexpectedly seized hostages at the U.S. embassy in Iran, Carter became paralyzed by the crisis, failed miserably in resolving the conflict, and lost the confidence of the American people and the election. Carter was bullied, and America lost because he did not stand up for the hostages or his nation.

In the business world Herb Kelleher of Southwest Airlines provides an excellent example of a leader whose company rose to the top of an industry because he stood up to a host of bullies. Southwest had an inauspicious beginning. Sued by competing airlines from the moment it incorporated, Southwest was not even able to fly for four years. But Kelleher, who was also an attorney, waived his legal fees and personally fought court battles against Continental, Braniff, and Trans Texas all the way to a victory in the Texas Supreme Court. Kelleher would have to fight off other airline attempts to nip his maverick airline in the bud, and today Southwest stands as one of the few successes in the airline industry. His example demonstrates the importance of standing up for your organization and principles. Successful leaders resist bullies no matter how long the odds.

PUSH BACK

And then there are quite simply times when a leader must show what he or she is made of. The first daytime German bombs struck London in August of 1940 at a moment when the Air Ministry had planned to hit Leipzig. But Churchill had another idea. He ordered his Chiefs of Staff to strike Berlin: "Now that they have begun to molest the capital, I want you to hit them hard, and Berlin is the place to hit them."

Churchill believed retaliation essential, especially when the Nazis attacked civilians. He invested the struggle with a sense of justice and nobility. "We will mete out to the Germans the measure, and more than the measure, they have meted out to us," Churchill said in a speech largely for Hitler's ears during July of 1940. "You do your worst, and we will do our best."

Churchill more than held his own with another fearsome dictator, Joseph Stalin. In August of 1942, after a series of exhausting and hazardous flights, Churchill arrived at the Kremlin for his first meeting with Stalin. The dictator was furious that the Allied forces could not launch more offensives against the Germans to take pressure off the Eastern Front. He began to taunt and bully Churchill, questioning the British resolve, demanding to know, "When are you going to start fighting?" Churchill crashed his fist on the table and launched into one of his wonderful, spontaneous orations. He told Stalin exactly what his feelings were about fighting. The interpreter struggled to keep up, and Stalin, without waiting for a translation, replied, "I do not understand what you are saying but, by God, I like your sentiment."

On his return to his villa Churchill dictated a telegram to Clement Attlee, his Deputy Prime Minister, deprecating Stalin's rudeness and lack of appreciation for all of Britain's efforts. Churchill announced he was ready to pack up and leave if Stalin's attitude did not improve. The British ambassador had been listening to his dictation and warned that the room was certainly bugged, that every word would be translated and sent to Stalin. This only incensed Churchill more. We do not know for certain whether Stalin received a copy of Churchill's heated remarks but we do know that at the next meeting between the two leaders, Stalin turned on the charm and expressed his gratitude for all that Britain was doing.

The lesson for modern leaders is that you have to stand up for yourself. There are times when you must answer force with force. And there can be strength in stepping away from the table when someone is out of line. A leader does business on his own terms.

TEAM UP

Churchill wisely recognized that the most effective way of dealing with a bully is through a powerful alliance. In May 1936 Churchill wrote to an advocate of appeasement, Lord Londonderry, who had recently made the mistake of meeting Hitler: "British policy for four hundred years has been to oppose the strongest power in Europe by weaving together a combination of other countries strong enough to face the bully. Sometimes it is Spain, sometimes the French monarchy, sometimes the French Empire, sometimes Germany. I have no doubt who it is now. . . . It is thus through the centuries we have kept our liberties and maintained our life and power."

Corporations have long recognized the importance of striking strategic alliances in the face of a bully. Even the most capable of leaders often have to seek support before a hostile meeting to solidify support and cover their flanks. And one of the primary reasons companies merge or enter into cooperative agreements is to do their share of pushing rather than being pushed about.

In the years before World War II Churchill backed or advocated several alliances and demonstrations of force that would at least have hindered, and possibly derailed, Hitler's efforts. Churchill knew the smallest European states could repel Hitler as part of a "Grand Alliance," if only Britain would stand behind them. He urged Britain to stand by Czechoslovakia against aggression, as France had declared it would do. Churchill envisioned the power of Britain and France acting as one. Note in the following address to Parliament how well Churchill foresaw the complexity of the problem; that even if the issues switched from one of defense to one of war, the alliance would be valuable. "Treat the defensive problems of the two countries as if they were one. Then you will have a real deterrent against unprovoked aggression, and if the deterrent fails to deter, you will have a highly organized method of coping with the aggressor."

CHANGE COURSE

When Hitler threatened Czechoslovakia, an unlikely opportunity appeared. Russia made overtures to France and Britain to form an alliance. Remarkably, Churchill set aside his personal hatred of Bolshevism and the Russian regime. Like other great leaders he recognized that the larger threat outweighed lesser considerations. He urged the British government to push for a Franco-Russian pact. Instead, the British government, set on appeasement, foolishly warned France it wanted no part of such an agreement. Churchill tried another tack. He went to Downing Street and told both the Prime Minister and the Foreign Secretary to warn Germany "that if she set foot in Czechoslovakia we should be at once at war with her."

They sent no such warning, of course, stuck as they were on a fatal course of satisfying Hitler's ever-increasing appetite. But Churchill anticipated how the game was rapidly changing, how appeasement was no longer an option. He told the press that it was a mistake to think that only one country was at risk. He knew Europe's borders and recognized that the fall of a strategic state would release many German divisions for use elsewhere. "It is not Czechoslovakia alone which is menaced, but also the freedom and the democracy of all nations. The belief that security can be obtained by throwing a small State to the wolves is a fatal delusion. The war potential of Germany will increase in a short time more rapidly than it will be possible for France and Great Britain to complete the measures necessary for their defence."

Indeed, as a Nazi attack on Czechoslovakia loomed, Churchill became the unlikely lightning rod for Russian military support for France and Britain. On the eve of the crisis fifteen senior Conservatives met at Churchill's flat in Morpeth Mansions, "passionate," as Churchill wrote, to "get Russia in." Even Churchill was "impressed" by how dramatically the Tories had "cast away all thoughts of class, party, or ideological interest."

True leadership ignites the nobler and more practical side of men and women, and leads them to reject the status quo.

LAY GROUNDWORK

Against long odds Churchill was making progress in mobilizing members of Parliament to take steps to isolate and encircle Hitler. History records, of course, that he was not immediately successful. Neville Chamberlain foolishly and tragically rejected the hand of Russia, as he had earlier turned down an offer from President Roosevelt to confer on the deepening crisis. Manipulated like a puppet, Chamberlain was seduced by Hitler's draconian terms at Munich, betraying the Czechs to the Nazis and making World War II inevitable.

Churchill may have lacked the political platform to create the military alliances the world needed to stop the bully in his tracks in the 1930s, but it is a mistake to think his efforts were in vain. Alliances take time to form. Just as a corporate executive must lay the groundwork for later cooperation, so, too, was Churchill readying Britain and its allies for the future. He was also gaining a crucial understanding of his enemy.

Unlike Chamberlain and others, Churchill expected the unexpected in Hitler. That became one of his secret weapons against one of the most fearsome and brilliant bullies of all time. For a brief, bloody age, Hitler appeared to be the master of chaos, and Churchill's recognition of the dictator's unusual tactics prepared him for the battles that lay ahead. Later he would write perceptively about Hitler's series of seemingly irrational moves in the late 1930s: "His genius taught him that victory would not be achieved by processes of certainty. Risks had to be run. The leap had to be made. . . . To wait till everything was ready was probably to wait till all was too late. . . .

KEEP BULLIES OFF BALANCE

Today's leaders can learn much from the stance Churchill took toward Hitler's actions and speeches. Churchill was keenly aware of the dynamics of personal and political power, and many of the principles he applied were classic and apply equally to modern business and politics.

From the outset Churchill put the Führer on the defensive. In the summer of 1932, while visiting Munich, Churchill met Ernst Hanfstaengel, a former classmate of Franklin D. Roosevelt at Harvard. Hanfstaengel was close to Hitler and implied to Churchill that the Führer would welcome a meeting. The rendezvous seemed all but settled, except for one fact. Churchill let the man know that he found Hitler's racist views repugnant. "Why is your chief so violent about the Jews?" he asked. "What is the sense of being against a man simply because of his birth?" The remarks were probably repeated to Hitler because the next day Churchill was told the meeting was off.

Over the years Churchill rarely allowed Hitler to gain the upper hand in their political and military duel. By the mid-1930s Churchill had seen that every leader who sought compromise with the Führer came out with the short end of the stick. Hitler's idea of negotiation was to dictate terms. Those who came hoping to reach a compromise were generally worn down by his threats and bullying and relinquished more than they ever imagined they would. They often grossly mistook Hitler's charisma for integrity, as Chamberlain did after he met Hitler in Munich. The Cabinet minutes record Chamberlain's thoughts, "The Prime Minister thought he had established some degree of influence over Herr Hitler. He was also satisfied that

Herr Hitler would not go back on his word once he had given it to him."

Churchill was far more discerning and quickly saw the danger Hitler represented. "There is no doubt that Hitler had a power of fascinating men, and the sense of force and authority is apt to assert unduly upon the tourist," Churchill wrote, recounting how he himself had rejected two invitations to meet with the Führer because he lacked the full authority of the British government. "Unless the terms are equal, it is better to keep away."

It's a lesson worth remembering. When facing a bully in business or politics, fight your battles on home turf and on your schedule.

HAVE THE LAST WORD

In speeches, broadcasts, and articles, Churchill landed rhetorical blow after blow against appeasement. His points were deft, his facts deadly accurate. Churchill was careful not to exaggerate, but every time Hitler broke a treaty or his word, every time he threatened another nation, Churchill rose up to point out why he was not to be trusted and needed to be stopped. After Churchill warned of Hitler's threat to the democracies of Austria and Czechoslovakia, the dictator exploded in a personal tirade against Churchill. Hitler asserted that he would never "allow any such foreign schoolmasters or governess to interfere with [the German regime]."

Hitler's ranting had the effect of elevating Churchill's stature at home and abroad. Churchill mastered the golden rule when it comes to crossing swords with a bully. Whatever the argument, whatever the issue, he always seemed to have the last word: "I am surprised that the head of a great State should set himself to attack British Members of Parliament who hold no official position and who are not even the leaders of parties. Such action on his part can only enhance any influence they may have, because their fellow-countrymen have long been able to form their own opinions about them, and really do not need foreign guidance."

Great leaders keep their cool and do not descend to responding to personal attacks. Churchill's stature only grew. The British public, military, and Members of Parliament were increasingly impressed by Churchill's ability to get under Hitler's skin merely by words. In time Hitler's reactions became symbols of Churchill's integrity, winning the statesman millions of supporters in Britain and abroad.

While fighting the biggest bully of them all, Churchill did far more than simply maintain his dignity. He steadily increased his public stature, until finally it became clear to the nation that he alone was the leader with the strength to stand up to Hitler. It's a lesson from which every leader can learn.

CHURCHILLIAN PRINCIPLES

- Stand up to people through your resilience and flexibility. Remember Andrew Carnegie's famous maxim, "Boss your boss just as soon as you can."
- Keep your enemies close. Study opponents and enemies in advance so you can anticipate their moves.
- Disarm enemies before they become too powerful.
- Co-opt support when opposition to your leadership stirs.
- Keep bullies off balance with your humor and sense of dignity. Do not take attacks personally.
- The best response to an outrageous insult is often silence. Let the weak squabble.

CHAPTER 6

Touch the Troops

Now I became the man on the spot. Instead of sitting at home waiting for the news from the front I could send it myself. This was exhilarating.

> —Winston Churchill, *The Second World War: The Hinge of Fate*, 1950

———

Churchill loved being in the thick of things: on the front line, visiting anti-aircraft defenses, cheering up bombed-out civilians, or meeting the troops and generals on whom the outcome of the war depended.

What makes his legacy particularly valuable for future leaders is how he did this at so many different levels of responsibility. In World War I Churchill dropped from First Lord of the Admiralty, the political head of the world's greatest navy, to commander of an infantry battalion of less than a thousand men in the trenches. After service at the front he returned to high and wide-ranging responsibility in a newly created post, Minister of Munitions. In World War II he had to be content with the Admiralty once again before becoming Prime Minister. Yet through all these very different positions his modus operandi remained essentially the same. Leaders lead, and Churchill never hesitated to take charge of a situation by leading from the front.

Decades before Tom Peters coined the phrase, "managing by walking around," Churchill was on the move—leading, managing, and motivating by maintaining personal contact with every element of his responsibility. Today many executives spend most of their time in aircraft and airports, shuttling from city to city to meet people and to keep everyone on their toes. As First Lord of the Admiralty before the outbreak of World War I, Churchill spent much time on an aquatic version of the corporate jet, the *Enchantress*, the Admiralty yacht with a complement of almost two hundred officers and sailors. Beginning in the fall of 1911, over the next two and a half years, Churchill spent a quarter of his days afloat.

He inspected warships, submarine depots, destroyers, and dockyards in Britain and abroad. The trips built morale and reinforced the impression that here was a First Lord who knew that the navy was about the sea. Sailors liked Churchill and found him engaging and approachable. Like some of today's best business executives, he was just as comfortable with the lower deck as he was with admirals. Part of leading is simply to be seen, to be out there, to be engaged. The *Daily Express* reported that during a visit to a submarine, "He had a yarn with nearly all the lower deck men of the ship's company, asking why, wherefore and how everything was done. All the sailors 'go a bundle on him', because he makes no fuss and takes them by surprise. He is here, there, and everywhere."

Churchill was doing more than simply mixing with the men. Leaders cannot always rely on the reports or impressions of subordinates whose views will be colored by their own inclinations. Leaders need to see things for themselves and like any executive in a new post, Churchill was gaining a firsthand sense of a fresh set of problems. Leaders are passionate. They reject the routine and dive headlong into operations. Churchill's visits helped him discover and implement immediate improvements. After a week at Portland docks, for instance, he ordered the sort of economy typical of a tough executive. Having discovered ships were being repaired and refitted simply to create work, he stopped the costly, wasteful practice. "Probe, Prune, Prepare," Churchill gleefully wrote Clementine, "one cannot do too much of it."

Unstructured visits can offer another benefit: a chance to find out what people need to excel in their work. Churchill's trips gave him a firsthand feel for the life of a sailor. General Patton wrote of the importance of generals' making themselves available to junior officers and ordinary soldiers, of going to them, instead of waiting to hear about a problem after the event. Churchill was not so different from an executive visiting a regional sales office or a call center in a distant city. Leaders use these trips to do more than ferret out problems; leadership is about more than cutting costs or slicing away bureaucracy. Churchill also used his trips to bolster morale and improve working conditions. After a tour of Harwich, for instance, Churchill ordered onshore amenities remarkable for their time: a recreational center with a bowling alley and reading room, a football pitch, and an authorized place to sleep "so that the men have proper places to go when spending the night ashore." He also pushed through increases in sailors' pay. Churchill used these visits not only to eliminate waste and remedy defects. He was keenly aware of the need to find ways to support and motivate sailors.

During World War II Churchill carried on with the practice of seeing things firsthand and ordering improvements where possible. He got results because he was approachable and open to change. "Informality is critical to candor," write Bossidy and Charan in *Execution*. "It invites questions, encouraging spontaneity and critical thinking." In July of 1940, for example, Churchill visited Britain's coastal defenses with General Montgomery. Monty gave Churchill an afternoon tour along thirty miles of coastline, but interestingly it was not during the formal part of the tour that the important business was done. Churchill suggested Monty have dinner with him and it was then that the General was able to air his problems. He thought it "curious" that his division, the only division "fit to fight any enemy anywhere" was immobile. Monty did not want to be strung out along the coast; he needed to be concentrated inland and mobile, able to mount a counterattack if the Germans invaded. And he knew how to do it: with ordinary civilian buses.

The next morning Churchill fired off an Action This Day minute. "I was disturbed to find the 3rd Division spread along thirty miles of coast, instead of being, as I had imagined, held back concentrated in reserve, ready to move against any serious head of invasion. But much more astonishing was the fact that the infantry of this division, which is otherwise fully mobile, are not provided with the buses necessary to move them to the point of action." Churchill concluded his memo with a firm instruction "that the GOC 3rd Division will be told today to take up, as he would like to do, the large number of buses which are even plying for pleasure traffic up and down the sea front at Brighton."

Leaders do not allow good ideas to gather dust in the inbox. Little more than twelve hours passed between dinner in Brighton and the Action This Day minute. Monty got his buses, though, as he wryly noted in his memoirs, he did not "know what the War Office thought." What is perhaps most instructive about this story is that it shows how the strongest leaders make themselves available for impromptu meetings and welcome unusual ideas. Churchill's gift was that he seemed to enjoy it even more and pressed harder for action when a proposed solution from the troops was both out of the ordinary and marvelously simple.

Throughout World War II Churchill would find time for such meetings with his generals, both planned and spontaneous. Weather, bad health, enemy fire—none of these could get in the way of his need to maintain regular physical contact with his troops and military hierarchy. Leaders do not wait for invitations to hop a plane or board a ship. As we shall see in Chapter 11, Forge Alliances, Churchill even applied his "touch the troops methodology" to creating and nourishing alliances with Franklin Roosevelt and Joseph Stalin. Leaders take the initiative and set the pace of the agenda.

THE VIRTUAL OFFICE

Regardless of his job, Churchill made a practice of getting out of his office to seek and resolve problems. The best executives are restless and eager to confront whatever difficulty gets in their way. In World War I, as the Minister for Munitions, Churchill frequently commuted to the front in the morning, returning to his London office to toil through the night. These Channel crossings were dangerous as well as taxing. One plane flipped after takeoff, requiring an emergency landing; still another caught fire, and Churchill himself crashed one of his aircraft. But whatever the risks, leaders have to go to the source of the problems.

In 1918 a memorandum from Churchill to the Prime Minister noted, "If we are to obtain any effective superiority in numbers it can only be by American aid." He went on to point

A LEADER ON THE MOVE

A demanding overseas tour in 1944 during which Churchill—in his late sixties—visited the troops, met with major military and political leaders, and still continued to direct wider events with his steady flow of minutes, telegrams, and letters.

August 11—Arrives by air in Algiers at 6:30 A.M. Discussions with the British resident minister, Alfred Duff Cooper. Flies to Naples. Stays at Villa Rivalta with General Wilson, Supreme Allied Commander Mediterranean. Conducts late-night discussions with Wilson and Harold Macmillan, the British resident minister with Allied Headquarters Mediterranean. Retires at 12:30 A.M.

August 12—Works on papers. Meets with Marshall Tito of Yugoslavia concerning future of region. Attends lunch in his honor. Swims at the island of Ischia. Meets with the Ban (governor) of Croatia, Dr. Subasic. Approves memorandum to Tito. Retires at 12:45 A.M.

August 13—Works on papers. Takes launch to Capri for picnic and swim. Returns to Naples in the afternoon to review naval convoy preparing for invasion of Riviera. Grabs twenty-minute nap in the launch. Attends another meeting with Tito and Subasic. Retires at 12:45 A.M.

August 14—Works on papers. Swims. Flies to Corsica. Embarks on HMS *Scotsman*. Attends dinner and discussions aboard HMS *Largs* with General Wilson; Admiral Cunningham, the Allied Naval Commander Mediterranean; General Eaker of the U.S. Air Force; and Robert Patterson, the U.S. Under-Secretary of War.

August 15—Embarks on a destroyer, HMS *Kimberly*, to observe the invasion of the Riviera.

August 16—Returns to Naples. Discusses future operations in Greece with Air Marshal Slessor and General Gammel. Swims. Has dinner and discussion with Macmillan on Russian policy in Poland.

August 17—Visits Monte Cassino with General Alexander, the

Allied Commander Italy. Flies to Alexander's headquarters at Siena. Dines with Alexander and General Harding.

August 18—Bad weather frustrates plans to visit front line.

August 19—Goes to Cecina to meet General Mark Clark, commander of the U.S. 5th Army. Visits 5th Army units. Visits Leghorn to see progress of rehabilitation of harbor. Flies to Naples. Dines with Generals Alexander and Harding and Admiral Cunningham. Retires at 3:30 A.M.

August 20—Flies to visit British front line on River Arno. Returns to Naples.

August 21—Flies to Rome. General Brooke and Air Marshall Portal arrive from London. Discussions with Sir Noel Charles (the British ambassador), Macmillan, Wilson, Brooke, and Portal on forthcoming British operations in Greece and the Allied role in governing Italy.

August 22—Day of political discussions, "Trying to unravel the tangle of our affairs here." Lunches with Italian prime minister, Bonomi, and his predecessor, Marshal Badoglio. Discussions continue until 1:00 A.M.

August 23—Audience with Pope. Meets Italian cabinet. Flies to Alexander's headquarters in Siena.

August 24—Visits New Zealand Division.

August 25—Works on papers at headquarters. Flies to 8th Army headquarters at Monte Maggiore.

August 26—Observes launch of new offensive. Visits front line close on heels of advancing troops. Approaches within five hundred yards of enemy positions from which machine-gun fire is coming: "The time I heard most bullets in WWII."

August 27—Flies to Naples. Takes Prince of Piedmont's launch to swim off the island of Pocida. Dinner and conference on future operations in Greece. Retires at 3:00 A.M.

August 28—Works on papers. Takes final swim in Bay of Naples. Flies to U.K. Pneumonia recurs. Temperature reaches 103 on landing.

September 5—Sails aboard *Queen Mary* for Quebec conference with President Roosevelt.

out that the American troops depended upon British munitions production for their fighting efficiency. His visits to France as the American reinforcements arrived enabled him to argue his case more forcefully than if he had operated only, or even mainly, from London. His regular visits to military headquarters also enabled him to assess priorities for the delivery of armaments and led him to set up munitions factories on the continent. Often he spent a few days in France at the modern-day equivalent of an executive apartment, a "charming room" at the Château Verchocq, placed at his disposal by the British Commander-in-Chief.

Churchill was an early practitioner of the virtual office. Wherever he might be—at the front, cruising on the *Enchantress*, or crossing the Atlantic to confer with Roosevelt—Churchill remained in control just as much as if he had remained in Downing Street. The necessary staff traveled with him. Telegrams continued to be dispatched and received. When he was Prime Minister during World War II, a mobile map room accompanied him. Wherever he went, whatever the purpose of his travels, and no matter what additional burden they imposed, the engine on which all depended kept churning ahead.

Before World War II Churchill entertained an amazing array of guests at Chartwell, including members of Parliament, intellectuals, and Professor Frederick Lindemann—Churchill's favorite scientist, "the Prof." As World War II loomed, the guest list bulged with senior officers and those ministers who recognized that Churchill was the only man strong enough to stand up to the Nazis. This was an important forum for Churchill, an opportunity to discuss serious issues in a comfortable, homey environment. It was also an alternative setting in which

Churchill could exercise leadership, where he could flesh out ideas, float parts of tomorrow's speech, and match wits with bright minds. Churchill was an intensely human man and needed, like all the best leaders, this casual, social contact.

Once he was Prime Minister, Chequers became his official weekend country house. However, it was easily identifiable by enemy aircraft, especially at night when the moon was up. Churchill's weekends were therefore sometimes spent at Ditchley, a large manor house in Oxfordshire. It belonged to Ronald Tree, a member of Parliament whose American wife had written to Churchill saying, "It is convenient for you at any time no matter how short the notice—it is at your disposal." Whether it was at Chequers or Ditchley, Churchill's arrival on Friday afternoons became an important part of his modus operandi. Here, without the constrictions of the London bunkers, he could assemble an audience around the dinner table. His brilliance inspired his guests (high ranking officers, ambassadors, ministers, family, and other interesting people). The conversation was a catalyst that encouraged ideas, while the whole occasion clearly boosted Churchill's own morale. After dinner there was frequently a film for relaxation.

It's a practice worth imitating. You can profit in all sorts of ways by inviting key staffers with their partners to your house rather than your office.

But Churchill's relaxed encounters were not only about establishing rapport with colleagues. Ordinary men also played a part in these weekends, men fighting the war, men with problems that needed solving. For these men a weekend could provide access to a Churchill who was far more flexible than other heads of government, most of whom dined only with a select inner circle. Churchill made it a point to welcome new faces and ideas.

Just as an impromptu aside to Churchill during a tour of a warship might spur action, so could a word to Churchill after a glass of brandy be effective. And you did not have to be General Eisenhower. In the fall of 1940, talking to Churchill about the Hurricane fighter, Wing Commander J. R. Kayll mentioned that a single incendiary bullet in the fuel tank was usually fatal. "A few months later," Kayll recalled, "I was sent to see a demonstration of a bullet proof petrol tank which shortly after was put into production."

Openness in leaders cuts both ways. Known for his receptive ear on military needs, Churchill was often invited to tour facilities or to examine new technologies. He was like the modern executive with a reputation for engaging in local problems whom the regional vice president invites for a visit knowing something useful will come of it. In June of 1939 when Churchill still had no official position in government, Kingsley Wood, Secretary of State for Air, took him around a new radar installation. Impressed by the technology, Churchill wrote to Wood on the need for protecting the radar towers more than a year before the first Nazi bombers arrived.

The lesson is simple. Receptive guests are welcomed back. Encourage give-and-take in your enterprise.

ENCOURAGE THE TROOPS

Whatever the primary motive, a visit by Churchill also improved morale, both for those visited and the visitor. Life can be lonely at the top and by getting out and about a leader is refreshed. Little could stop Churchill when his presence was needed. More than once he flew when the weather was hazardous or his health suspect. Indeed in January 1941 he had planned a trip to Scapa Flow to see Lord Halifax off to his post as ambassador in Washington but was in bed with a heavy cold. A blizzard had struck Scapa, and Churchill's doctor forbade the trip. But the bulldog could not be stopped. "What damned nonsense!" Churchill exclaimed to his doctor, tossing off his bed clothes. "Of course I am going."

The truth was Churchill needed these expeditions. During a visit to the 1st Anti-Aircraft Division and an experimental rocket site, he happened upon some action. Antiaircraft guns were furiously blasting away at incoming German bombers. Churchill nearly had to be dragged away for the next stop on his tour. "This exhilarates me," he said. "The sound of these cannons gives me a tremendous feeling."

That may sound downright boyish, but leaders often exhibit a sense of wonder for the action and inner workings of their organizations. They find ways to have fun and share a little camaraderie. While crossing the Channel back to England with the Prime Minister and several prominent members of the War Council in early 1940, Churchill abandoned his colleagues, who were keeping largely to themselves. The First Lord of the Admiralty sipped port with the officers in the wardroom then descended to the lower mess decks. "Eventually [we] found him on the stokers' mess deck," recalled the Gunnery Officer, "sitting on a mess table swapping yarns." When a mine was spotted in the ocean, Churchill sensed an opportunity for a little fun. He suggested to the captain that they blow it up by gunfire. They did, scoring a bull's-eye, the pieces raining all around. Everyone seemed cheered by the little adventure.

Throughout World War II Churchill gave countless addresses to hundreds of thousands of troops. Churchill loved to take the stage, as he did in June 1943 when he spoke to thousands of troops in the Roman amphitheater at Carthage, later joking, "Yes, I was speaking from where the cries of Christian virgins rent the air whilst roaring lions devoured them, and yet I am no lion and certainly not a virgin."

Of course, Churchill regularly addressed Parliament and broadcast during times of crisis, classic ways of maintaining touch with the nation. But leaders have to do more than give staged speeches. Churchill often found a way to mix informal visits with these set occasions.

Churchill surprised many by his unannounced visits to the smoking room in the House of Commons. Like an executive eating in the cafeteria or loitering at the water cooler, this was Churchill's way of demonstrating his accessibility. He acted as if he were a backbench Member of Parliament, not the leader of the nation. He'd sip whiskey and water, chew on his cigar, and read the newspapers as if he had nothing better to do. Members gathered around and he was peppered with questions. Once, one of the Members talked of the public thirst for bombing civilians in Germany as revenge for the London raids. "My dear sir," Churchill replied, "this is a military and not a civilian war. You and others may desire to kill women and children. We desire (and have succeeded in our desire) to destroy German military objectives. I quite appreciate your point. But my motto is 'Business before Pleasure.'"

Leaders do not become prisoners in ivory towers. Try exercising your authority in all sorts of surroundings. You'll likely expand your reach and power.

Yet even the best leaders have to be reminded at times of the value of their words or presence. Consider the story of how during the summer of 1942, Julian Amery, a young officer just back from the fighting in Egypt, came to Churchill's room at Downing Street and told him of dispirited soldiers. Amery suggested Churchill go to the scene. Churchill was puzzled, wondering what effect he could possibly have. "What should I do out there to improve morale?" Amery knew exactly what the Prime Minister should do. Visit and talk to the troops and officers. "It would," he said to Churchill, "have an electric effect."

When times are rough, a leader can often make a difference simply by being there.

PAY ATTENTION

Leaders touch the troops by paying attention and noticing little things that make a difference in people's lives. When Churchill led a battalion at the front during World War I he brought enthusiasm and fresh insights to his posting. Just months before, as First Lord of the Admiralty, he had headed the entire British navy. The debacle of the Dardanelles had changed all that. Now he had to show what he could do with less than a thousand men.

There is little more impressive than a leader who can touch the troops and motivate people when his fortunes are low. Churchill had an uphill battle. As a soldier he had no experience of trench warfare. The 6th Battalion Royal Scots Fusiliers had suffered severe casualties and many were not eager to have Churchill replace their commanding officer. More than a few wished the "fallen politician" had been foisted upon another battalion.

His first step was to throw himself into his new command.

At the French village of Moolenacker near the front, he began by paying attention to the ordinary needs of his men. "Gentlemen, we are going to make war on the lice," he announced to his battalion, leaping into an animated history of the vermin and, as one officer recalled, "its importance as a factor in wars ancient and modern." The lecture was followed by action. Churchill formed an antilice committee and arranged for brewery vats to be brought to Moolenacker and for the delousing to begin. The troops were impressed. "It was a terrific moment, and by God it worked," recalled one officer.

You can touch the troops by demonstrating your enthusiasm and willingness to learn about new problems. Churchill took instruction in bomb throwing and machine gunnery. He also showed he understood the dire circumstances in which men found themselves and earned a reputation for compassion, letting a troublemaker go free after learning he had fought at the bloody battle of Loos.

Churchill wisely realized his men needed to be entertained if he was going to rebuild their morale for the fighting ahead. He was in some ways like a company executive making sure his workers had enough diversions to keep them relaxed and upbeat. Incredibly, he organized games—everything from pillow fights to obstacle races, which were followed by a concert and dinner. "I think they want nursing & encouraging more than drill-sergeanting," Churchill wrote to Clementine. "Such singing you never heard. People sang with the greatest courage who had no idea either of words or tune. Poor fellows, nothing like this had ever been done for them before. They do not get much to brighten their lives, short though they may be."

When Churchill's battalion reached the front, he made for the trenches and took it as his duty to make them safer. He had clever, practical ideas for improving shelters and dugouts and, most important, for adapting the parapets so they would actually stop bullets. No detail was too small for his scrutiny. "Instead of a quick glance at what was being done, he would stop and talk with everyone and probe to the bottom of every activity," recalled Lieutenant Jock MacDonald, echoing the "probe" and "prepare" method Churchill had instilled at the Admiralty. The men took to Churchill, realizing that he was doing everything in his power to keep them alive. In this manner he demonstrated that he was as much a part of this life-and-death struggle as his men. He diligently walked the thousand yards of trenches three times a day; at night he often accompanied a fellow officer out of the trenches on patrol into no-man's-land, risking his own life more than once. "The Hun machine guns opened up, belly high," one of his officers recalled. "Why the hell we weren't killed I just don't understand."

Word of Churchill's efforts reached home. "I think that everyone has heard of the improvements you have effected in your battalion," Clementine wrote. "Soldiers back from the front on leave talk about it." Brave, resourceful, and fully engaged, the lieutenant colonel who had first called himself "the escaped scapegoat," became so popular that some of his men pinned up his photograph in the trenches.

Leaders touch the troops by becoming one with them, by sharing their risks, by lightening their burdens, and by anticipating their problems. Churchill demonstrated his leadership by caring about every aspect of life in the 6th Battalion Royal Scots Fusiliers, from the lice that added to the men's discomfort to the reinforced trenches that could save their lives.

Leaders cannot afford to be pompous if they hope to touch the troops. On the other hand, they need to arm themselves against the subordinate who takes advantage of the open door and becomes overfamiliar. Never forget the power of humor, as Churchill demonstrated in the margins of a World War II conference. A meeting had just adjourned when Lieutenant Colonel Vernon Kelly noticed an intoxicated GI in the doorway. Addressing the Prime Minister, the soldier said, "Hey Fatso. Where's the men's room?" To this Churchill replied, "Turn left down the corridor to the second door on the right. The sign on the door says GENTLEMEN but don't let that deter you."

CHURCHILLIAN PRINCIPLES

- Tour the entire organization to get a personal and firsthand sense of daily operations.
- Do not rely on reports from subordinates.
- Leave the guided tour and rub shoulders with the men and women doing the work.
- Build morale by having fun and spreading optimism in your visits.
- Share some of the problems faced by your staff and workers. Listen and respond to valid complaints and suggestions.
- Improve the work environment.
- Ferret out excessive bureaucracy and waste. Demand initiative and solutions.
- Lunch with colleagues and subordinates to gain a relaxed sense of workers and problems.
- Leaders have no office hours. Work flows seamlessly into the rest of life.

CHAPTER 7

Turn Details into Action

Is it really necessary to describe the Tirpitz *[German battleship]
as the* Admiral von Tirpitz *in every signal? This must cause a
considerable waste of time for signalmen, cipher staff and typists.
Surely* Tirpitz *is good enough for the beast.*

—Winston Churchill to the First Lord of the Admiralty,
January 27, 1942

Churchill was a man who mastered details without losing
sight of the larger picture. His mastery enabled him to direct, drive, and inspire the many artists needed to tackle an
enormous canvas. He needed to know the progress of countless complicated operations. He wanted to know production
figures, delivery dates, forecasts, and statistics. His search was
seldom about quarterly reports. Churchill often wanted answers by the end of the week, if not by the end of the day.

Churchill made things happen by relentlessly pressing for
facts and details. As Bossidy and Charan write in *Execution,*
"Only the leader can make execution happen, through his or
her deep personal involvement in the substance and even the
details of execution." On the day he was once again appointed
First Lord of the Admiralty in 1939, Churchill instituted a
working style that would continue when he became Prime
Minister. His method was based on the minute, a dictated note
to obtain information, initiate discussion, issue instructions,
or propose action. The minutes would go to his professional
advisers or cabinet colleagues. They could be as short as a sin-

gle sentence or as long as necessary to convey an argument. They could be witty or weighty or contain encouragement, praise, or rebuke. Several thousand were sent in the course of each year. Because many ended with the phrase, "Pray let me have," they became known in the Admiralty as "First Lord's prayers."

Many were designed to elicit the information Churchill needed to grasp a problem. The first, on September 3, 1939, was typical of many to follow, asking for specific information: "Let me have a statement of the German U-boat force, actual and prospective, for the next few months," Churchill wrote to the Director of Naval Intelligence. "Please distinguish between ocean-going and small size U-boats." Another minute that day requested figures on how many rifles and mines the navy possessed; another asked what escorts would be provided for a planned large convoy. Churchill's best were targeted and admirably blunt. A few months later a minute concerning food imports reminded the recipient that he wanted no "point of view . . . just the cold-blooded facts."

To urgent minutes, Churchill attached a red label carrying the instruction printed in capital letters ACTION THIS DAY.

PUT IT IN WRITING

Leaders of all kinds recognize the central role of written communication in leading and managing large operations. Despite the importance of personal contact, a request for information in writing concentrates the mind of the recipient. Conversation is discursive, "but there's something about putting your thoughts on paper that forces you to get down to specifics," Lee Iaccoca wrote. "In conversation you can get away with

ACTION THIS DAY

ACTION THIS DAY

Most immidiate

52

Admiralty to F.O. Narvik. Most immediate.

Begins. First Lord to Lord Cork, personal and private.

Should you consider that situation is being mishandled it is your duty to report either to me personally or to Admiralty upon the situation and what you would do yourself (stop). You should of course inform the General of the action you have taken, so that he will have an opportunity of expressing his views to the War Office.

all kinds of vagueness and nonsense, often without even realizing it."

Churchill entered into a written dialogue with his staff. His minutes were very much like formal e-mails, though in general they were to be taken more seriously and acted upon with greater urgency than anything in the Internet age. Churchill's facility for dictating made it easy for him to send minutes covering complex subjects in many fields. His written word spurred people into action. He frequently sent ideas to his "colleagues for consideration, for criticism and correction," in the hope that he would promptly "receive proposals for action in the sense desired." His minutes were always to the point and demanded straightforward replies. "Let us not shrink from using the short, expressive phrase, even if it is controversial."

Churchill's method was about creating an environment that emphasizes actions and results. Take a look around. Is there a way you could introduce something like Action This Day memos to your organization? Could you create a color code to rank the importance of e-mails or memos?

Churchill did more than send minutes on specific problems. He also wrote on the larger picture facing the navy: the strategic information systems any executive needs to do his or her job correctly. For example, when Churchill took office early on in World War II, U-boats were sinking increasing numbers of British merchant ships. Churchill responded to the crisis by dictating a minute on the need for a situation room with maps, charts, and ample staff. Within weeks, he had a nearly real-time picture of the threats facing the navy. The period library in Admiralty House was transformed into a War Room, with pin-dotted maps showing the position of British, Allied, and enemy ships around the world. It was manned twenty-four hours a day and the maps in the War Room were curtained off to prevent the unauthorized from seeing any secrets. Not only was the staff constantly updating the positions of vessels on the maps, but reports were continually generated on attacks, right down to the tonnage sunk.

There is an old saying that a business leader needs to feel the heartbeat of a company. Churchill tried to be at ground zero, as close to the action as possible. He slept on the floor directly above the War Room and was known to start his day with a visit a little after seven in his colorful dressing gown. If news came of an attack during the night he was often down in minutes. No other government department had anything like the War Room. When a crisis struck, Churchill and his staff could get a visual snapshot and promptly take action. Captain Richard Pim, who created the map room and who would go on to run Churchill's map room when he became Prime Minister, explained, "If a raider was reported in any specific area we were able in a few moments to say what British ships were in its vicinity and what was their speed so that a wireless signal could be sent ordering them, if necessary, to alter course to avoid the danger."

It isn't just war that creates complicated challenges. How might you create a War Room for your organization?

Great leaders are hungry for strategic information about their organizations or businesses. They aren't satisfied with the way things were done before. Within a month of becoming First Lord, Churchill demanded the creation of a Statistical Branch, which, characteristically, he called S Branch. Its purpose was to group all Admiralty statistics and present them to him "in a form increasingly simplified and graphic." He detailed his requirement in a minute, "I want to know at the end of each week everything we have got, all the people we are employing, the progress of all vessels, works of construction, the progress of all munitions affecting us, the state of our merchant tonnage, together with losses, and numbers, of every Branch of the RN and RM [Royal Navy and Royal Marines]. The whole should be presented in a small book." He continued by explaining that it was a method he had employed as Minister of Munitions in World War I when each week "in an hour or two I was able to cover the whole ground, as I knew exactly what to look for and where."

Churchill was doing what good leaders do, creating methods to systematically gather and then display information. But there was nothing passive about the process. The key, as Collins noted in *Good to Great*, was that this new department "outside the normal chain of command" would feed him "continuously updated and completely unfiltered—the most brutal facts of reality." Armed with these daily details he could ask further questions—and demand results.

Churchill's War Room and "small book" gave him both a nearly real-time view of operations and weekly updates on all important statistics. The War Room, like the modern technologies of cell phones, pagers, computer networks, and e-mail, made possible many of the advantages of round-the-clock work. If Churchill noticed a wayward ship somewhere around the world that might be intercepted by Nazi raiders, he was not above ringing up the Minister of Shipping in the middle of the night to solve the problem.

At times the naval staff was overwhelmed by Churchill's requests for information and results. But even his critics recognized he was uncovering problems that needed immediate attention. In modern vernacular he had a way of "drilling down." After only his first week in office he discovered, to his astonishment, that not a single ship in the navy was equipped with radar. He immediately minuted the appropriate admiral that the technology should be installed in all naval ships, adding, "those engaged in U-boat fighting is of high priority."

FINDING PROBLEMS, GETTING RESULTS

Churchill's frequent visits to naval ports often spawned a series of minutes on specific problems. He was like the visiting executive discovering departments that had neglected their core mission or overlooked a critical weakness. Churchill's second visit to Scapa Flow with the Commander in Chief resulted in a memo urging the immediate camouflaging of oil tanks and the creation of dummies to distract German bombers. In a visit to Portsmouth Churchill discovered that most of the nation's radar and wireless research was vulnerable to a single air strike and suggested moving elsewhere whatever research did not need to be conducted in the area. Churchill's minutes brought tangible results. A special protective net was redesigned to cope with the latest torpedoes. On his third day at the Admiralty, Churchill dictated a minute on whether it might be possible to fool the enemy with dummy warships in naval ports to "draw long exhausting and futile attacks upon worthless targets, while the real ships are doing their work elsewhere."

Churchill's visits to naval facilities, frequent minutes, and information systems provided the raw knowledge he needed to identify and solve problems. If information was Churchill's lifeblood, orderly written communication was his means of tracking a huge number of widely varying problems. His minutes ensured that tasks were given the appropriate priority, an approach many modern leaders might find valuable in an age when e-mail has become so overused that many fail even to scan most of their messages.

Minutes could be tough, confronting failures and exhorting the recipient to redouble efforts, like this one to his friend and adviser Professor Lindemann: "You are not presenting me as I should like every few days or week with a short clear statement of the falling off or improvement in munitions production." But near the end of every minute, Churchill always made clear that however bleak the situation, he had suggestions about possible solutions. He was doing more than introducing a sys-

---

CHURCHILL'S MINUTES

Churchill's minutes pressed for the facts and details necessary to produce action.

May 24, 1940

Professor Lindemann

Let me have on one sheet of paper a statement about the Tanks. How many have we got with the Army? How many of each kind are being made each month? How many are there with the manufacturers? What are the forecasts? What are the plans for heavier Tanks?

---

tematic approach to solving problems. He was working to turn around an organization that had fallen behind the times.

Churchill did more than seek answers; he provided them himself. Sometimes the responses were to entirely new questions, such as those that arose when a new tank gun was introduced; other times they were novel solutions to standard problems, such as how to reduce the time lost in commissioning and refitting warships. In the case of the tank gun, there was no clear policy on whether all the new larger guns should go into tanks on the production line or whether some should be used to replace the smaller, much less effective guns in existing tanks. In a five-hundred-word minute dated April 3, 1942, addressed to the Ministers of Production and Supply and the Chiefs of Staff, Churchill analyzed the problem and concluded that the argument for putting all the new guns into new tanks was "overwhelming." Reading the minute one wonders why there had been any doubt. Less than a month later, when HMS *King George V* was due for a refit and a new ship, HMS *Anson,* was being commissioned, Churchill provided the answer in a single paragraph: "Let the whole of the *King George V* crew go on leave simultaneously for a fortnight. Meanwhile let the *Anson's* crew be transferred to *King George V,* and the *King George V* men go as a complete, integral, highly trained unit to the *Anson,* which is an identical ship in almost every aspect. Thus the working up of the *Anson* would consist almost entirely of testing her material qualities. This change ought to save at least a month's or six weeks' delay in the ship being ready for battle."

MAKE ACTION A GOAL

Churchill's approach to business and problems valued action and progress. When a staff member wrote a report that Churchill found to his liking, Churchill often replied in red ink and shorthand "v.g. press on." Forward momentum was the key. "It was like the stone thrown into the pond," wrote the Deputy Director of the Trade Division, "the ripples go out in all directions, galvanizing people at all levels to 'press on', and they did."

Once a course of action was agreed upon, Churchill saw no reason to delay. He was racing like an entrepreneur to be first to market. Anything was possible if one worked hard and fast enough. New committees and organizations were formed in a day. Initiatives were taken on problems that had seen no progress for months. Mañana was alien to Churchill's vocabulary. Churchill went to bed so late, often two or three in the morning, that nearly an entire day's work could be devoted to an issue first raised in the late afternoon. "He finished everything before he went to bed," recalled Colonel Ian Jacob. "And, of course, he nearly finished us." There is an entertaining story from late in the war when Churchill was Prime Minister. During a series of meetings with Roosevelt in Canada, the President's Secretary of State, Cordell Hull, made the mistake of trying to call it a night. Churchill was appalled that he would think of sleep. It was only midnight. "Why man," he exploded, "we are at war!"

Churchill managed such outrageous working hours by routinely refreshing himself with an hour's sleep late in the afternoon and by having relief teams of secretaries and aides on call at any time of day or night.

He disdained bureaucrats who dithered out of fear or an institutional reluctance to take action. "Very fine arguments are always given for doing nothing," he was later to write. Early in the war, Churchill had suggested floating mines down the Rhine to retaliate for the German magnetic mines that were wreaking havoc with merchant shipping. The Air Staff's response questioned the international legal status of such a proposal and concluded that retaliation might be "unprofitable" because of counterreprisals. Next to the conclusion Churchill wrote mischievously, "Don't irritate them dear!"

When something important slipped through bureaucratic cracks, Churchill always found the time and energy to obtain the details necessary for remedial action. In September of 1940 critical war supplies due from the United States were unexpectedly delayed. Churchill intervened directly. He phoned the chairman of the purchasing board, Arthur Purvis, and requested a daily report on when various arms would be released and when they were scheduled to ship. These detailed telegraphs enabled Churchill to monitor this complex problem and reduce delays, even though he was on the other side of the Atlantic.

Churchill was the quintessential man of action. Indeed, one of his supreme achievements as a leader was to make action an explicit, conscious objective. Churchill did not just have AC-TION THIS DAY labels and standard ministerial boxes. He had an "O" box into which he collected minutes on offensive actions that he hoped to take. So, too, did he collect and befriend men of action to recharge his spirit. When the exploits of an officer struck him as particularly bold, Churchill invited him to Admiralty House so that he could hear the dramatic tale firsthand. Some of these men became Churchill's friends and were later invited to Chartwell. Of course, the most noticeable symbol of action was Churchill himself. The pace of work visibly picked up when the bulldog was in. As his secretary Kathleen Hill said, "When Winston was at the Admiralty, the place was buzzing with atmosphere, with electricity. When he was away, on tour, it was dead, dead, dead."

Vitality and rigorous work habits help make great leaders. But they can also be an Achilles' heel. Sometimes Churchill took on too much work and expected what seemed the impossible from his staff. Of course, the *Fortune* 500 is filled with countless executives who occasionally share this tendency. Andy Grove was known for the iron discipline he demanded at Intel. Nor would anyone suggest that Bill Gates drove Microsoft to its dominant position by being nice or expecting less than the maximum. The reality is that leaders must set high standards.

Churchill did not have the latitude of a modern business executive, who is able to fire large numbers of incompetents. Britain's civil service and armed services certainly had their share of less than able people, and it would only be natural that some bureaucrats and career officers occasionally resented Churchill's novel methods and demand for results. What is interesting is that most of those who went to work for Churchill soon came to realize that he set the bar high to provide the necessary goals. Though he hoped for quick results, what he expected was action and signs of progress. Nor was his mind fixed. "If one experiment proved unsuccessful, another was suggested," wrote his Parliamentary Secretary Geoffrey Shakespeare. "The only unpardonable sin was to sit back and accept the seemingly inevitable."

His Private Secretary John Colville wrote that "patience was a virtue with which he was totally unfamiliar. His anger was like lightning and sometimes terrifying to see, but it lasted a short time. He could be violently offensive to those who worked for him and although he would never say sorry, he would equally never let the sun go down without in some ways making amends or showing that he had not meant to be unkind." Elizabeth Layton, a secretary who worked in Downing Street and accompanied Churchill on many of his journeys to America, Russia, and the Middle East, said of him, "He would never be one to take a dislike for no reason. He is a most warm-hearted person and infinitely loyal to his friends." She noted that having incurred his wrath over a typing mistake she was rewarded by a compliment a few minutes later, "Oh, very good indeed, how quick you were."

The lesson is that you'll earn people's loyalty no matter how hard you drive them provided that they know their efforts are appreciated.

"UTMOST FISH"

Churchill's ability to get someone going on a problem was extraordinary. As a cabinet minister he quite rightly never saw himself as limited to speaking only on his specific responsibilities. He had views on almost everything and was never shy about airing them. He had very definite views on waging war and followed nearly every aspect of it. A fellow cabinet minister noted, only a month into World War II, that Churchill had "a very big position in the country" and that he was "the one popular figure in the cabinet." His wide-ranging activities did not endear him to colleagues who feared his increasing influence, but his behavior was consistent with a practice followed by the best modern leaders. Those in charge reject artificial barriers. It really does not matter what you call it. It is simply looking beyond the traditional limits of a job or division to further the needs of an organization. Leaders instill the sense that initiative and willpower can solve any problem.

Some of the most amusing tales of Churchill at work are also the most enlightening for today's leaders. The story of the Action This Day minute that he directed one morning at his Parliamentary Secretary illustrates how adroitly Churchill leaped barriers: "I am concerned about the shortage of fish. Parliamentary Secretary will immediately take up the matter with the ACNS [Assistant Chief of the Naval Staff] and the head of the Mine Sweeping Division to see if any trawlers can be released for fishing. We must have a policy of 'utmost fish.' Parliamentary Secretary will report to me by midnight with his proposals."

Geoffrey Shakespeare was stumped. While the flagging fish supply was indeed a problem for wartime Britain, he knew nothing about fishing, nor did it have anything to do with him. No matter. He jumped to it and quickly convened a conference of trawler owners. By the end of the day, he was a fishing expert and began dictating a detailed recommendation for the "formation of a new Fishing Promotion Council" in which the Admiralty would play a key part. Shakespeare recalled that it was after midnight when he delivered his recommendation to Churchill, who, after peppering him with questions, "concurred in the formation of the new council and instructed me to constitute it forthwith." Miraculously, in the course of a very long day, Churchill had managed to spur one of his staff toward the solution to a complicated problem that no one had seemed to know anything about. As Shakespeare wryly wrote, "So a policy of 'utmost fish' was fostered by the Admiralty in war time."

It is easy to laugh but the lesson resonates especially loudly today. The important problems confronting modern leaders are not routine. Churchill was a leader because he could inspire others to solve difficulties they often imagined were beyond their range or capabilities. His enthusiasm and demand for action spread throughout the departments he led. For a nation that faced seemingly insuperable odds, it was vital to instill the attitude that any problem could be solved by a First Lord's prayer and persistent follow-through. Even the problem of "utmost fish."

CHURCHILLIAN PRINCIPLES

- Demand frequent, regular reports to keep your finger on the pulse of operations.
- Confirm oral instructions in writing.
- Keep thinking up new ways to gather and display key information about the progress within an organization.
- Tour throughout your organization down to the lowest level to gather a firsthand sense of what is working properly and what needs attention.
- Give urgent tasks priority through clear marking, along the lines of Churchill's ACTION THIS DAY labels.
- Be goal and action oriented. Press for results by the earliest feasible time. Do not accept bureaucratic excuses. Demand initiative and signs of progress.
- Seek out and promote workers, managers, and executives who get results; listen and learn from their examples.
- Show appreciation and you'll earn people's loyalty.

CHAPTER 8

Never Surrender

*Never give in, never give in, **never, never, never, never**—in noth-ing, great or small, large or petty—never give in except to convic-tions of honour and good sense.*

—Winston Churchill, speech at Harrow, October 29, 1941

———

We've talked before about the supreme challenge Churchill faced in May of 1940 during his first days as Prime Minister. In addition to preparing the British military and public for a German invasion, he had to convince a skeptical America that he would not cave in as the French had. All this while many in his own Cabinet and Parliament questioned his qualifications to lead.

Resolve and moral fortitude are at the foundation of leadership. They are put to the test only during a crisis, and, though you may be born with a certain amount of fire in your belly, you discover what you are made of only when you need it most. When dedication and commitment become married to a higher purpose they rise to what James MacGregor Burns calls "transforming leadership."

Leaders can inspire their followers only by leaping into the fray. Those in charge know that the greatest opportunity for leadership comes when times are hardest: when the company has lost its sense of identity; when management has just slashed jobs; when trusty markets have gone sour. This is the hour when a leader elbows into the battle.

In May of 1940 Churchill had an inauspicious start as

Facts Are Better Than Dreams

Prime Minister. His plea to Roosevelt for fifty idle U.S. World War I destroyers fell on deaf ears. The President's advisers, bearing in mind their London Ambassador's advice, feared that if they sent Britain the destroyers, they might quickly fall into the hands of the Nazis. Yet Churchill gave no hint of despair. When he spoke to his ministers, his words were visceral and defiant: "I have nothing to offer but blood, toil, tears, and sweat." That same day in Parliament, Churchill repeated the soon-to-be legendary phrase in his "victory at all costs" speech.

More than six decades later, in his book *Good to Great,* Jim Collins pointed to Churchill's wartime bulldog tenacity as a shining example of how modern business leaders must tackle challenges. "Churchill as you know," wrote Collins, "maintained a bold and unwavering vision that Britain would not just survive, but prevail as a great nation—despite the whole world wondering not if but when Britain would sue for peace."

Yet Collins was careful to note that Churchill never sugar-coated the truth or downplayed the long odds. "Churchill never failed . . . to confront the most brutal facts." He cemented his leadership by never failing to start with the hard facts no matter how daunting the situation. His demand for the unvarnished truth and his readiness to share it with fellow leaders and the public ensured that his integrity would be unquestioned. His winning combination was equal parts harsh reality and stubborn, measured optimism. Honesty and courage were the principal requirements. Churchill led like a seasoned prizefighter, prepared to take painful shots to the body for a chance for a jab or a hook that would chip away at his enemy's defenses.

Britain's situation was desperate. Yet Churchill called for victory, years before victory was possible, indeed when defeat seemed the more likely outcome. "You ask what is our aim. I can answer in one word: victory, victory at all costs, victory in spite of all terror, victory, however long and hard the road may be; for without victory, there is no survival."

In truth the battle hung in the balance. Of the hundreds of thousands of British and French troops trapped at Dunkirk, Churchill himself believed that fewer than 30,000 might escape. The garrison besieged at Calais was also awaiting evacuation by sea and Churchill made the tough decision to command these men to remain in order to keep the advancing

Germans at bay while the larger numbers at Dunkirk were ferried home. Incredibly, more than 300,000 British and French troops made it safely to Britain, carried across the English Channel by an armada of boats, naval and civilian, of all shapes and sizes.

Buoyed by the miraculous Dunkirk evacuation, Churchill delivered one of his most famous addresses to the House of Commons. What makes the speech especially relevant to modern leaders is how Churchill understood the importance of addressing a variety of audiences. He was faced with a challenge not that different from a company on the verge of bankruptcy. In such a circumstance, management must convince employees, partners, banks, and competitors that the company will rebound. So, too, did Churchill have to motivate or warn various groups. On this occasion he was speaking ostensibly to the British nation, civilian and military. But he was also sending a powerful message to Germany and Italy, for there are times when you must let your enemies know that you are not about to quit:

> Even though large tracts of Europe and many old and famous States have fallen or may fall into the grip of the Gestapo and all the odious apparatus of Nazi rule, we shall not flag or fail.
>
> We shall go on to the end. We shall fight in France, we shall fight on the seas and oceans, we shall fight with growing confidence and growing strength in the air, we shall defend our island, whatever the cost may be. We shall fight on the beaches, we shall fight on the landing grounds, we shall fight in the fields and in the streets, we shall fight in the hills; we shall never surrender."

Churchill was operating much like an executive who has just forged a delicate partnership in trying times. He had enlisted the support of the nation and put his enemies on notice that he would fight to the end. Now he needed to let his new ally, President Roosevelt, know that Britain would not fail. On February 8, 1941, after furious personal lobbying by Churchill, the crucial Lend-Lease Act was passed in the U.S. House of Representatives. The bill would grant Britain the war materiel and food supplies it depended on for survival. The following day, February 9, in a BBC broadcast, Churchill spoke directly to Roosevelt. "Put your confidence in us. Give us your faith and your blessing and, under Providence, all will be well. We shall not fail or falter: we shall not weaken or tire. . . . Give us the tools and we will finish the job."

What separates organizations is how they respond to adversity. Great companies "hit the realities of their situation head-on," writes Jim Collins. "As a result, they emerge from adversity even stronger."

SACRIFICE

The resolve and determination Churchill stressed in his wartime speeches entailed tremendous sacrifice, but through it all he made clear that every man and woman was engaged in a noble, great, and even joyful enterprise.

Leaders lead by example. Turning a faltering business around may not be as earthshaking as saving the free world from Hitler, but it, too, requires sacrifice.

John Maxwell has written of what he calls The Law of Sacrifice, of how leaders must make personal sacrifices to earn a following. Churchill certainly fit that description, risking his health and safety throughout the war by flying through hostile skies for critical conferences with the Allies. But he did something far greater than simply provide an example by his own dedication and fearlessness. In late 1941, when the war was going very badly, Churchill went to speak at his old school, Harrow. His uplifting words are worth studying for anyone who must lead during harsh times: "Do not let us speak of darker days, let us rather speak of sterner days. These are not dark days, these are great days, the greatest days our country has ever lived; and we must all thank God that we have been allowed, each according to our stations, to play a part in making these days memorable in the history of our race."

Churchill challenged a nation to find the strength and vision to look upon its current struggles as an opportunity for greatness for each and every man and woman. What goals do you have to instill your workers with a greater sense of purpose?

MEET FEAR

When things were darkest, Churchill did not hesitate to broadcast or address Parliament or his Cabinet. Consider how critical it was for America that President Bush gave an address from the White House the night of the World Trade Center attacks. The military had ordered the President to be shuttled around the country in *Air Force One*. But Bush was right to insist that he return to the White House and speak. When crisis strikes, leaders must rise to the occasion. Delay can be fatal to the resolve of a nation or an organization.

Churchill never hesitated. When the Germans invaded Russia in June of 1941, most experts, including the American ambassador in London, Joseph Kennedy, thought the Russians would be finished before the fall. Upon receiving the sobering news of the invasion on the morning of June 22, Churchill immediately told his Private Secretary, John Colville, to advise the BBC he would broadcast at nine that night. He spent the day preparing for the broadcast and then offered skeptical members of his cabinet odds of 500 to 1 "that the Russians are still fighting, and fighting victoriously, two years from now."

Leaders act swiftly. Churchill recognized the threat to Britain and the United States if Russia fell. He promised supplies to Russia and forestalled any wavering in his own administration. As Lord Beaverbrook, the Minister for Aircraft Production, later wrote: "It was a decision taken without calling his Cabinet together. It was a decision taken in the likelihood it would arouse a measure of hostility among sections of his own party. Nor could he have any guarantee either of the attitude of the British newspapers."

When things go terribly wrong, leaders should use the very chaos of a crisis as a galvanizing factor. Good managers or executives face this when they miss sales targets and get trounced by competitors. They must anticipate the concerns of management and workers. They must act decisively, guiding staff toward solutions.

In January 1942, when the news was blackest, Churchill demanded a vote of confidence from Parliament. A lesser man would not have tested his support and risked his position of authority, especially in an often fickle political forum. But Churchill sensed he could strengthen his leadership and the nation's resolve just when things appeared at their bleakest. It was only weeks after the attack on Pearl Harbor. Two British battleships had been sunk by the Japanese, whose forces had overrun Malaysia and were about to capture Singapore. And in

Washington the month before, Churchill had suffered a mild heart attack while visiting Roosevelt.

Vulnerable to critics, Churchill spoke on the third and final day of the Parliamentary debate: "Things have gone badly and worse is to come. In no way have I mitigated the sense of danger and impending misfortunes of a minor character and of a severe character which still hang over us. But at the same time I avow my confidence, never stronger than at this moment, that we shall bring this conflict to an end in a manner agreeable to the interests of our country, and in a manner agreeable to the future of the world."

The vote in his favor was 464 to 1.

PRAISE HEROES

Never in the field of human conflict has so much been owed by so many to so few.

Churchill's elegant phrase was first uttered to General Ismay moments after he had left one of the fighter control centers during the Battle of Britain. Hundreds of German aircraft had tried to destroy British planes on the ground. Airfields, docks, and factories were under furious attack. Nearly every British fighter had hurtled into combat, the nation's survival depending on their success. The British pilots rose heroically to the occasion, shooting down seventy-six German planes and losing only twenty-six fighters in aerial combat, although forty-seven were destroyed on the ground. Four days later in Parliament, Churchill repeated his tribute to Britain's fighter pilots.

Crises demand superior performance. An organization with its back against the wall depends upon an extraordinary effort from its people. Churchill may have been a harsh taskmaster and tough boss, but he understood the importance of praise in times of crisis. Though best known for his recognition of heroes, Churchill's wide acknowledgment of all, civilians and military personnel alike, was a potent factor in maintaining morale.

As Minister of Munitions, in the critical last years of World War I, while organizing the vast quantities of munitions that Britain needed, Churchill ensured that the workers toiling away from the limelight received their fair share of acknowledgment. In 1918 he told Parliament, "It is a striking fact that more than nine-tenths, and in many branches far more than nine-tenths, of the whole manufacture of the shells which constitute the power and terror of the British Artillery, are due to the labours of women, of women who before the War never saw a lathe."

Visiting the front that same year, he telegraphed the head of a Birmingham tank factory: "Express again to all hands my satisfaction at the admirable deliveries."

Although Churchill's words of praise, made informally day by day, were seldom recorded verbatim, some accounts exist. A typical example comes to us from his stop in Iceland on his return from meeting President Roosevelt in August 1941. One of the U.S. destroyers on loan to Britain, which were instrumental in protecting transatlantic shipping convoys, had been named HMS *Churchill* and happened to be in port. Churchill addressed the ship's company, telling them that hard times lay ahead, three years of war at least. But he reminded the sailors that they were carrying out one of the war's "most vital jobs." Yes, Churchill acknowledged, Britain had seldom faced bleaker times, but as one of those on board recalled, "he was confident that we would survive, and with right on our side and help from allies . . . we should win through to a great and glorious victory." Three cheers went up for the Prime Minister, and the sailors rushed to the ship's rails to cheer him on his way.

Leaders also recognize the importance of encouraging allies. Churchill's praise of American soldiers reached back to World War I, when he paid tribute to two divisions of U.S. Marines who took a heroic part in the defense of Paris. Churchill knew that history repeats itself and that Britain would again need its American cousins.

The most important lesson is to remember to praise widely when you are losing. That is when it counts. When times are rough make sure to encourage teams and individuals in the thick of it. Loyalty to your subordinates demands it.

STAY COOL

During the 1930s while Britain was burying its head in the sand in response to the growing threat from Nazi Germany, Churchill was accused of panicking when he warned Parliament of the dangers ahead. In reply he offered a basic lesson on meeting a crisis: "It is very much better to have a panic feeling beforehand, and then be quite calm when things happen, than to be extremely calm beforehand and to get into a panic when things happen."

Leaders must look and sound like leaders. Under the spotlight, they must have steady hands and resolute voices. They must project an aura of calm and confidence. As Napoleon wrote: "The first quality for a commander-in-chief is a cool head to receive a correct impression of things. He should not allow himself to be confused by either good or bad news." Things are seldom as bad or as good as they seem at first sight.

Churchill epitomized coolness under fire. He recommended sounding the air-raid sirens as little as possible so as not to panic a public subjected to frequent flying bomb attacks. "The PM said one must have sleep," noted Admiral Cunningham, "and you either woke well-rested, or in a better land!"

While dictating a telegram to Roosevelt a few days later, Churchill interrupted the message with an aside to the President: "At this moment a flying bomb is approaching this dwelling." The threat did not stop Churchill from continuing his dictation and moments later he inserted a second aside, "Bomb has fallen some way off."

Despite Churchill's nerve, he knew it was a mistake to be unreasonably macho. Leaders must balance resilience with compassion. For example, while Mayor Giuliani of New York was respected for his toughness, much of the international praise he received was for his compassion in dealing with the World Trade Center attacks. Churchill, too, was human and not afraid to show his emotions to his staff, family, and friends. He cried in front of his staff upon learning of British sailors who had gone down with their ships. Countless times he visited the catastrophic scene of the latest bombing attacks to demonstrate his compassion. Once a woman who had just lost her home saw his tears and cried, "Look, he really cares!" The crowd cheered, and what might have been a moment of despair instead became a celebration of British steadfastness.

It is a strange paradox. But just when events seem beyond your control is often the point at which you have the greatest chance of inspiring people.

Churchill allowed no disaster to overwhelm him. In the wake of a calamity, Churchill took an hour or two for reflection with his closest staff or family. Sometimes he simply needed to be alone: to absorb the blow before he could settle on the appropriate military and public response. In the spring of 1942, after the fall of Singapore, he went to his country home, Chartwell, to remember the seasons and his animals. He wrote to his son that his goose, which he affectionately dubbed his naval aide-de-camp, and the swan had been felled by a fox. Though Churchill had not visited Chartwell for months, his "yellow" cat made him aware of "his continuing friendship."

Sometimes the best response to a crisis is not to hit the SEND button or return the call, but to take a deep breath, talk to a confidant, or sleep on it. Act calmly and decisively in the morning.

SYMBOLIZE DEFIANCE

Churchill set the tone for a nation in conflict. He could take the abstract and bring it to life with visual metaphors. His first full World War I speech was a classic. Appointed First Lord of the Admiralty at the age of thirty-seven, he was entrusted with the most powerful navy in the world. But he spoke about far more than battleships in his call to arms at the Royal Opera House. Churchill was defining and celebrating the British character and spirit in terms every man and woman could understand, seizing upon something as tangible as the British bulldog. "The nose of the bulldog has been turned backwards so that he can breathe without letting go." His message was clear. Just as the bulldog does not let go in a fight, so, too, would Britain hold on no matter how long and hard the fight.

Three-quarters of a century later another great British political leader showed similar defiance when turning around

Britain's then flagging economy. After a decade during which trade union power had dominated the political scene, Margaret Thatcher stepped onto the stage as Prime Minister. Famously declaring, "The lady is not for turning," she plotted a bold course of economic recovery from which she was never diverted.

The lesson is clear. Make no bones about who you are and what you stand for.

Strong leaders recognize not only the importance of symbols of defiance but also their opposite, symbols of defeat. Churchill would not permit contingency planning for failure, knowing it would inevitably leak out and breed pessimism. Just weeks after becoming Prime Minister in 1940, Churchill was advised of a doomsday plan to be implemented in the event of a full-scale German invasion of Britain. The royal family and top members of the government would be evacuated to Canada. Churchill flatly vetoed the proposal, adding, "We shall make them rue the day they try to invade our island." Days later he replied in the same vein to the Director of the National Gallery concerning a similar proposal for the safety of paintings: "No, bury them in caves and cellars. None must go."

Leaders carry on. Ronald Reagan won enormous support for the grit he showed after being shot, though Teddy Roosevelt must take the cake on that score. He, too, received a bullet from a would-be assassin. But Roosevelt insisted on completing a scheduled speech before going to the hospital.

Churchill was cut from the same cloth. Just weeks after he had rejected plans to evacuate the royal family, the French government fled Paris. Surrender appeared certain. The weather was so bad that Churchill was warned not even to think about flying over to bolster French morale. "To hell with that. I'm going, whatever happens," he announced. "This is too serious a situation to bother about the weather."

Accompanied by General Ismay and Lord Halifax, the Foreign Secretary, Churchill landed near Tours at an abandoned airfield. There was no one to meet them so, announcing himself in his dubious French accent as the Prime Minister of Great Britain, he commandeered a taxi and declared to his companions, "Well, the journey does not promise well. Do you not think that a good luncheon is in order? The hotel in Tours used to have some admirable Vouvray in its cellars."

Lunch was not easy to find in a deserted Tours, but Churchill found a closed café and talked the proprietor into serving a meal. Soon the French Prime Minister, Paul Reynaud, appeared. But the French were too deeply demoralized for even Churchill to talk them out of surrender. Reynaud was certain the Germans would invade Britain. "What will you do when they come?" he asked. Privately, Churchill mused to General Ismay that the two of them might have no more than three months to live. But that, of course, is not what he said to Reynaud. "If they swim we will drown them. If they land we will hit them on the head, *frappez* them *sur la tête.*"

There is nothing like courage in the face of a challenge to inspire followers. Humor will also take you far.

CONFRONT DEFEATISTS

Churchill stamped out defeatism wherever it appeared, understanding it could spread like a wildfire if not confronted. He had no patience for gossips and quitters. After a particularly devastating round of bombing in June of 1940, Churchill called a secret session of the House of Commons. "Let us get used to it. Eels get used to skinning. Steady continuous bombing probably rising to great intensity occasionally, must be a regular condition of our life."

When times are rough, workers and competitors frequently spread half-truths about impending trouble, layoffs, cutbacks, and the like. Leaders must resolutely combat and defuse gossip with facts. In the spring of 1939 the defeatist U.S. Ambassador to Britain, Joseph Kennedy, started telling prominent people that the British would surrender to the Nazis. Walter Lippmann, the influential American journalist, passed on this gossip to Churchill at a dinner party. According to the Labour MP Harold Nicolson, the word "surrender" had barely been uttered when Churchill confronted the journalist. "No, the Ambassador should not have spoken so Mr. Lippmann; he should not have said that dreadful word. Yet supposing (as I do not for one moment suppose) that Mr. Kennedy were correct in his tragic utterance, then I for one would willingly lay down my life in combat, rather than, in fear of defeat, surrender to the menaces of these most sinister men. It will then be for you, the Americans, to preserve and to maintain the great heritage of the English-speaking peoples."

Sometimes a leader has to wage a campaign against complacency. Churchill faced such a situation in 1939. That fateful summer, as the Nazis prepared to invade Poland, Britain's Prime Minister, Neville Chamberlain, took the extraordinary step of adjourning Parliament for two months. Churchill warned the House of the danger and foolishness of going on "holiday" for August and September, "when the harvests have been gathered, and when the powers of evil are at their strongest." Leaders do not withdraw when disaster looms. "At this moment in its long history," Churchill continued, "it would be disastrous, it would be pathetic, it would be shameful for the House of Commons to write itself off as an effective and potent factor in the situation."

There was, of course, a political goal behind the untimely Parliamentary holiday. Chamberlain wanted to silence the opposition to his vain policy of appeasement with Hitler. The two-month break was passed by the House, but Churchill was anything but broken. "We can do no more," muttered a shattered young Conservative member of Parliament to Churchill. "Do no more, my boy?" Churchill roared back. "There is a lot more we can do. This is the time to fight, to speak, to attack!"

Leaders get people back to their posts and away from thoughts of failure. They do it without delay.

HONOR AND GOOD SENSE FIRST

Churchill did not compromise on issues of principle and never surrendered when it counted. But when circumstances changed, he was an extraordinarily practical man. Leaders fight wars, not battles. Though Churchill steadfastly insisted his generals had the determination to win, he knew how to handle defeat.

In early 1942, learning that Singapore island was threatened by the Japanese advance through Malaysia, Churchill ordered the mobilization of the "entire male population" in defense. In a telegram he advised General Wavell that he expected "every inch of ground to be defended" and "no question of surrender to be entertained until after protracted fighting among the ruins of Singapore City."

But three weeks later, when General Percival reported that

the troops were "incapable of further counter-attack," Churchill promptly gave the order for the British to surrender. In private he was not pleased. Wavell told him that the troops had fought poorly, without spirit, a revelation that disturbed Churchill deeply. Yet in his BBC broadcast that night from Chequers, Churchill spoke of the surrender only as an opportunity, as one step toward victory, "Here is the moment, to display that calm and poise, combined with grim determination, which not so long ago brought us out of the very jaws of death. Here is another reason to show, as so often in our long story, that we can meet reverses with dignity and with renewed accessions of strength."

Every business must overcome failure and defeats on the road to success. Strong leaders maintain their perspective. You take your knocks and get up. What counts is fortifying the morale of the men and women who must carry on tomorrow.

CHURCHILLIAN PRINCIPLES

- Symbolize defiance and confidence no matter how long the odds.
- Encourage and enlist the support of subordinates and partners when times are rough.
- Offer clear examples of sacrifice that inspire everyone within your organization.
- When things go wrong, act and speak promptly to consolidate your leadership.
- Praise individuals who demonstrate the qualities needed in the face of adversity.
- Confront defeatists and critics.
- Do not waste time on contingency planning in case of failure. If you think too much about what may go wrong you will inevitably fail.
- Balance resilience with compassion. The toughest leaders have a heart.
- Always show loyalty to your subordinates.

CHAPTER 9

Experiment

I knew nothing about science, but I knew something of scientists, and had much practice as a Minister at handling things I did not understand. I had, at any rate, an acute perception of what would help and what would hurt, or what would cure and of what would kill.

—Winston Churchill, *The Second World War: Their Finest Hour,* 1949

———

Churchill was a natural innovator. His fertile mind was open to new ideas across a huge range of subjects, from the workings of government to the realms of science, technology, and new weaponry. We've seen how in World War I he played a huge role in the development of the tank and naval aviation. He also helped modernize the British navy, introducing larger guns and converting from coal- to oil-fired ships.

To know the right questions to ask you need some basic knowledge. By reading voraciously, Churchill knew the history of warfare and weapons through the ages, as well as the latest fantasies from science-fiction writers such as H. G. Wells. Churchill's advantage was that he never feared asking what others might think a stupid or naïve question. He never fretted that he was not an expert, that his far-fetched ideas needed a good deal more development before they became of any practical use. "The details will work themselves out," he would say. Nor did he let criticism of his less cogent ideas impede his con-

159

CHURCHILL WAS OPEN

Churchill was willing to learn from anything, even enemy broadcasts.

October 6, 1939

Please see attached report of German radio interview of U-boat commander. . . . A conversation is arranged and then delivered with full effect, saying as much as possible without giving away what high authorities realise should be concealed. Now, why should we not develop the same method? . . .

Please go to the Ministry of Information with this minute from me and the copy of the broadcast in question, and see what can be done to keep our end up on the radio in this particular sphere.

Report results.

---

stant flow. A leader's role is to get things rolling, to push the first snowball down the slope.

BRAINSTORM

Decades before the buzzword had been invented, Churchill was a compulsive brainstormer. The many suggestions for improvements or changes he floated in his constant stream of minutes and meetings created a culture where what counted was thinking, trying, and testing. In the words of the two-time Nobel Prize winner Linus Pauling, "The best way to get a good idea is to have a lot of ideas."

Churchill showed how an informed layman can be a skilled

and powerful proponent of technology. In other words, you don't need to be technically savvy to bring the strengths of technology to your enterprise. While Churchill literally seemed to burst with ideas, his greatest strength was that he recognized his limitations. Well before World War II, he struck up his friendship with the remarkable Professor Frederick Lindemann. By the early 1930s, Lindemann had become Churchill's technical and scientific alter ego. As part of the Churchill entourage, Lindemann accompanied him on visits to military installations and became a regular at Chartwell and, when Churchill became Prime Minister, at Chequers. Though an odd couple on the surface, Lindemann was anti-social and a vegetarian, they were a perfect team. Whereas Churchill disliked technical and scientific jargon, Lindemann could, as Churchill's private secretary John Colville put it, "simplify the most opaque problem, scientific, mechanical or economic." Churchill came to rely on what he called Lindemann's "beautiful brain" to explain the most technical problems.

By the time Churchill headed the Admiralty at the outbreak of World War II, Lindemann had become an integral part of his team. Lindemann helped digest and focus the daily mass of statistical and technical information. A statistician in the Admiralty noted that "Churchill felt that he wanted an independent mind to digest and criticize these papers. It was not enough, amid the heavy pressure of his duties, to have a cursory knowledge of matters outside his province; he wanted to have a deeply critical knowledge, and what better person to aid him towards getting that than the Prof."

As the war progressed Churchill granted Lindemann unfettered access to the most secret documents, everything from the latest classified research to enigma decrypts. In turn, Lindemann offered piercing insights on a wide range of weapons, technologies, and matters of production. Some have faulted Churchill for sending on some of Lindemann's draft memos essentially unchanged, as if the ideas were his own. But what was important was that the ideas circulated.

Wise leaders ally themselves with talented, technically astute people to spark experimentation and innovation in their organizations. Churchill made it a practice to pursue and maintain working relationships with both scientists and the heads of various technical departments, who were engaged in the most critical research and development for the war. In the case of radar, for example, which played such a vital role in Britain's air defenses, Churchill learned of the first successful experiments in 1935 while a member of the Air Defense Research Sub-Committee. Though years away from becoming the wartime Prime Minister, he quickly became a staunch advocate of radar, befriending the technology's inventor, Robert Watson-Watt. Incredible as it sounds today, in 1936 the Air Ministry was ambivalent about the fledgling technology. Watson-Watt's research was frustrated by a lack of government funding. For help the inventor turned to Churchill, who, though holding no official position at the time, pressed for a meeting with the Prime Minister, at which he urged more resources be focused on the "potent discovery."

Leaders sometimes mistakenly take a hands-off attitude toward research and development, spawning separate, isolated fiefdoms with little accountability. Churchill's stubborn personality seldom let that happen. He took a personal interest in the men engaged in research and ensured that promising innovations and developments were kept on track.

By the fall of 1940 Churchill had the authority to make

radar a key element in Britain's defense. He assigned its future development the "very highest priority" in a note to the War Cabinet, making it absolutely clear what was needed. "This demands Scientists, Wireless Experts, and many classes of highly skilled labour and high-grade material." And he put in perspective the significance of the effort. "On the progress made, much of the winning of the war and our future strategy, especially Naval, depends. We must impart a far greater accuracy to the AA [anti-aircraft] guns, and a far better protection to our warships and harbours. Not only research and experiments, but production must be pushed hopefully forward from many directions, and after repeated disappointments we shall achieve success."

Churchill understood an important principle for every leader fostering innovation: plans must be balanced realistically against the unpredictability of the innovation cycle. Experiments and research would not suffice. Churchill needed results on projects as tangible as more accurate anti-aircraft fire. Yet he was fully aware that many obstacles would have to be overcome before he could achieve his objective.

CELEBRATE INNOVATION

Nearly every business faces pressures—a last-minute technical hitch on a product or service or the sudden need to cleverly counter a competitor's market strategy. Churchill did more than bring an intense focus on goals. He showed in spades how to marshal teams to meet a technical challenge during a crisis. He knew how to create and inspire what today we would call a hot group.

Innovation works best when it lives in an enterprise. Take

the case of the disturbing news that confronted Churchill at the Admiralty in the fall of 1939. The loss of three merchant ships to underwater devices could not be explained as being caused by traditional mines. An investigative committee soon unlocked the secret: the ship's own magnetic fields were triggering the explosions.

Britain's lifeline for food and war materiel was threatened. The toll from the magnetic mines mounted: five merchant ships were sunk on November 19 alone. Churchill marshaled a team to counter the enemy's new secret weapon. On November 20 he gathered his admirals and advisers at a late-night meeting at the Admiralty. Convoy routes were changed and sea and aerial patrols added in an endeavor to catch the mine layers. Plans were made for technical defensive measures—sweeping with electrical currents or towing a "skid" to set off mines. Two days later Churchill suggested creating a "special section" to learn everything possible about the mines, to find them, and to search for a solution. On November 23 the section was in business, and that very night a couple of naval officers found and successfully disarmed a magnetic mine stuck in the low tide.

Fostering a culture of innovation and experimentation is about more than technical know-how. It is about bringing passion to your business and nurturing an environment that celebrates discovery and achievement. The following night Churchill orchestrated an elaborate show in the Admiralty's cinema room. He put the men and the mystery mine in the spotlight. Lieutenant Commander Lewis, one of the officers who had plucked the mine from the mud, took center stage. Churchill recalled, "I gathered together eighty or a hundred officers and officials in our largest room, and a thrilled audience

listened to the tale deeply conscious of all that was at stake."
By making it a performance Churchill elevated the discovery
and inspired the countless men who would have to unravel
the technical challenge. Churchill ran the show, probing with
his usual detailed questions, concluding famously, "to sum
up, you have dissected this monster, divided it into pieces and
now you can examine it at leisure."

The show infused the task with a sense of glory and nobility. Celebrating the discovery of the mine, Churchill praised
the courage of Lieutenant Commander Lewis and his colleague. By spreading the excitement and joy of the discovery of
the Nazis' secret weapon to nearly a hundred men, Churchill
increased everyone's dedication to finding a solution. It's a lesson worth remembering. The next time you're wondering how
to regain your edge, remember that nothing works like a simple passion for excellence. Give the men and women engaged
in the hard work of your biggest challenges in innovation a
chance to shine.

By December 1, 1939, possible solutions began to emerge.
The following week in Churchill's room, word came that there
had been success in reducing "to one third of its original
amount" the magnetic field of a trawler by demagnetizing
it with an electric coil around its hull, "degaussing." The next
week Churchill listened in his room to the news that a trawler's
magnetic field had been reduced yet further. "We think we
have got hold of its tail," he excitedly told Roosevelt in a
Christmas Eve telegram, adding the following day in a letter to
Chamberlain, "it looks as if the demagnetization of warships
and merchant ships can be accomplished by a simple, speedy
and inexpensive process."

The search to counter the magnetic mines took nearly

three months, the task heightened by the daily pressure of increasing numbers of ships sunk by U-boats. Leaders create a framework for studying and solving problems. Churchill's inspirational backing and his natural inclination to celebrate the discovery of the first mine undoubtedly helped spur and speed the eventual solution.

KEEP ON TRACK

As the war progressed and Churchill became Prime Minister, he developed a system. Each day he worked through locked dispatch boxes of telegrams, parliamentary questions, reports from the Chiefs of Staff, documents needing signatures, and what were termed periodical returns.

Churchill was passionate about the need to develop and quickly produce new weapons to beat the Germans. Periodical returns might include statistics on deliveries, manpower, or the latest bombing attacks. They also included reports on new technologies or developments, for example, the latest news on an idea Churchill and Lindemann had been enthusiastic proponents of before the war: "smeller," a radar that could be fitted within an aircraft to track an enemy plane. Smeller was a great success, and showed the speed of innovation under Churchill. By June of 1940 only the most preliminary experiments had been carried out. Yet by October Churchill learned to his delight that during a couple of hundred nighttime skirmishes Smeller had a 75 percent success rate in tracking and intercepting enemy aircraft.

Leaders have to be more than enthusiastic backers of experiments and research. When innovations do not proceed on schedule, they must root out the stumbling block. Innovation

---

CHURCHILL'S TECHNICAL INITIATIVES

Over the course of his political career, Churchill was a major inspiration for many technical innovations, such as:

Formation of the Royal Naval Air Service

Improved aircraft controls and instruments

The tank

Artificial Mulberry harbors: prefabricated harbors made of caissons anchored offshore to facilitate logistical support for the Normandy beaches in 1944

Radar, including Smeller night-fighter radar and radar in warships

---

is like countless other creative processes. Sometimes it needs prodding. When Churchill learned, for instance, that a long agreed-upon improved design for bombsights had not progressed for months, he minuted Lord Beaverbrook: "I would be very glad if you would look at the files and ascertain who was responsible for stifling action."

Early in the war Churchill approved the development of a radar-controlled searchlight called Yagi. It was but one of many emerging radar-related technologies, which also included GL, a direction finder for antiaircraft guns. When in September of 1940 Churchill discovered to his dismay that there had been numerous setbacks in the technology's development, he immediately minuted Lindemann: "What has happened: & What can be done?" Bureaucratic infighting was the cause: a couple of squabbling ministers. Churchill did not delay. He transferred both radar projects to Lord Beaverbrook, the Minister for Aircraft Production, whom he had learned to trust.

Innovation is about more than encouraging a culture of experimentation. Research and development have to maintain a robust pace. Churchill's constant demand for progress reports reduced the chance of a new weapon or defense system falling through the cracks because of insufficient resources or the wrong minister at the helm.

CHAMPION INNOVATORS

Perhaps the most critical role a leader can play in encouraging a culture of innovation is to identify, promote, and support talented individuals, scientists like Watson-Watt and Lindemann, as well as talented executives like Lord Beaverbrook. In August of 1940 Churchill, much impressed by the initiative and talent of Major Jefferis, head of the army's experimental establishment, decided the man deserved a promotion. "I regard this officer as a singularly capable and forceful man who should be brought forward to a higher position. He ought certainly to be promoted to lieutenant-colonel as it will give him more authority." The army balked. A hundred and forty-nine majors were in line to be promoted before Jefferis. Age and service outweighed talent in the army's system. Churchill knew better, writing, "It is important to bring able men forward in war time, instead of deferring entirely to seniority." Jefferis not only got his promotion; Churchill moved his department to the Ministry of Supply, both to ensure he had all the resources he needed and to bring his work under the direct eye of Lindemann. Soon Jefferis's work was overseen by the Minister of Defence, Churchill himself.

The major the army had not wanted to promote rose to major general. In the first year that Churchill shepherded its efforts, Jefferis's group designed and produced in massive quantities several new important weapons, including the sticky bomb, puff ball, bombard and long-delay fuse. When others hesitated over a technical problem, Churchill put Jefferis on to it.

Quite literally, Churchill got a bang out of Jefferis. Innovation is about the search for inspiration and achievement. Leaders who produce results promote, protect and support talented individuals, regardless of age or title. They know that the project leader on a hot team may not be the oldest or the one with the most experience. Indeed, finding, promoting, and protecting rising stars may be the most critical task of a leader.

CHURCHILLIAN PRINCIPLES

- Ask questions about how processes and technologies might be improved. You don't need to know all the answers, just the right questions to ask.
- Encourage a culture where what counts is thinking, trying, and testing.
- Align yourself with an expert who can help advise you on new ideas and innovation.
- Launch teams to tackle innovation projects.
- Celebrate the men and women engaged in your biggest innovation challenges.
- Champion innovators and protect them from bureaucrats.

CHAPTER 10

Build Hope and Confidence

It is one thing to feel confident and it is another to impart confidence to people who do not like your plan and who feel the same confidence in their knowledge as you do in yours.

—Winston Churchill, Parliament, June 10, 1925

Churchill knew how to boost the morale and confidence of a nation under fire. He had what General Patton called his battle face, the rare ability to never let down his spirit or guard in front of the troops, the nation, or the enemy. But more than that, Churchill was blessed with an affirmative quality modern leaders admire. He exuded hope and confidence.

Creating hope in those who have every reason to be downcast requires far more than an aura of toughness. People naturally fear hard times and sudden change. Yet Churchill proved that with the right leadership, men and women can be inspired to greatness by difficult times. Churchill not only saw reasons for hope and confidence in the darkest days of World War II but was able to infuse his unique combination of stoicism and optimism into the very backbone of the nation, the armed services, and his own staff. As Leo Amery, a minister in Churchill's government put it, "No one ever left his cabinet without feeling himself a braver man."

Ten years after the war, Churchill modestly played down his own contribution to winning when he said, "It was the nation and the race dwelling all round the globe that had the lion's heart. I had the luck to be called upon to give the roar." But it was Churchill's roar that called the British people to action. Great leaders bring out the inner strength that people often do not know they possess. The British are a hardy people with a long history of warriors, but it was Churchill who brought out their most admirable qualities when the nation's survival depended upon them. He gave each and every man and woman a heroic role to play, and they rose to the challenge, dedicated and ready to make every sacrifice.

That is the heart of leadership.

CONTAGIOUS CONFIDENCE

Inspirational leaders are beacons of hope. They project an aura of confidence and resolve that is quite literally contagious. Churchill had this gift. So did Roosevelt, Truman, Patton, John F. Kennedy, Martin Luther King, Jr., and more than a few of today's business leaders. They are charismatic. They inspire followers and they get things done. "The leader must have infectious optimism, and the determination to persevere in the face of difficulties," said Field Marshal Montgomery, a man in whom Churchill had great confidence. "He must also radiate confidence, even when he himself is not too certain of the outcome. The final test of a leader is the feeling you have when you leave his presence after a conference. Have you a feeling of uplift and confidence?"

Churchill met this test of inspiration on many different levels. Beyond his speeches, there was his presence: his beaming smile and bulldog glare, his defiance, and, of course, his physical and mental energy. Churchill's spirit was seldom crushed. The morning after the first night of the Blitz, Churchill drove to ground zero: London's East End and the docks. An air-raid shelter had taken a direct hit, with dozens killed and more wounded. Churchill's car pulled up amid the chaos. "It was good of you to come, Winnie," the crowd called out. "We thought you'd come. We can take it. Give 'em it back." It was to become a rallying cry.

That first blitz visit set the tone for dozens more. Churchill brought his V for victory sign, his cane, his tears, his words of strength. Leaders go straight to the front line, and Churchill often arrived while the ruins were still smoldering. When he called out to the crowd, asking if they were disheartened, they cried back, "No!" Churchill had come to feel the nation's pain, to give the people the resolve they would need to face the months and years ahead.

CALM DEFIANCE

Leaders find many ways to inspire confidence. Churchill did more than visit the scenes of devastation after a raid. When bombers threatened he also frequently displayed a cavalier disregard for his own safety. Shortly after a War Cabinet meeting during the summer of 1940, Churchill was chatting with his friend Brenden Bracken in the garden when an air raid siren warned of an approaching raid. They kept drinking as everyone else hurried to the nearby shelter. When the Blitz began, Churchill took immediate precautions to move ministers and officials to safer offices. Yet he stayed on at Number 10, an ancient and vulnerable building, and did not move into a properly reinforced headquarters and bedroom until more than a week of bombing had passed. Even then he was famous for being the last one to go to the shelter. Indeed, when the bombs dropped, more often than not he clambered up the staircase and popped out onto the roof for a better view. On one occasion those left below suffered in a smoke-filled room until someone ventured out to discover the Prime Minister sitting on the chimney. Churchill's enthusiasm for seeing the action was abundantly clear to his staff, colleagues, ministers and important visiting American diplomats. Leaders meet the enemy head on, and Churchill gave those around him the impression that he was ready, indeed eager, for the fight.

Churchill's calm defiance of the dangers of the nightly air raids and his regular visits to those rendered homeless by the latest attack infused his leadership with a sense of camaraderie. He had the rare gift of being able to inspire nearly everyone around him, from the troops to the generals, managers and factory workers. People felt that he was one of them. Found in one of the pockets of the siren suits he had made to order was this endearing message: "May God grant you the very best of health and strength to carry us through our Greatest Ordeal in History to keep the British Empire free." The signature read, "From British Workers."

The lesson is clear. Engage yourself in the day's conflicts. Take risks. Boost the confidence of your organization by making sure everyone knows you are all in it together.

LEAD WITH FACTS

Churchill's defiant optimism was about more than his soaring rhetoric and sonorous phrases. Motivating people during a crisis is often a delicate, two-step process. Before the confidence-building stage of the dialogue, you must first tell it like it is. Good leaders are especially careful not to underestimate the hardships and obstacles that must be overcome. You earn trust by soberly confronting the task before you. Otherwise you may fall prey to the other extreme, paralyzing workers with an image of the insurmountable.

Many leaders in politics and business fail to grasp this essential process. For example, during the terrorist attacks of September 11, many American leaders failed to realize the importance of this critical first step. Top officials initially underestimated the threat of anthrax. The House Majority Leader, Dennis Hastert, shut down Congress for days while postal workers were told to keep working and not bother being tested for exposure. Sadly, the nation's sense of trust and fairness was tried when two postal workers died. There seemed to be a double standard: one for Congressmen and Senators, another for common workers. That was a mistake.

At the other pole were the alarmists. More than a few would-be American leaders panicked, turning vague terrorist warnings into unfocused public alerts that frightened the populace. Between these two poles stood Mayor Giuliani of New York in what proved to be his finest hour. The Mayor showed his pain and tears for the thousands of victims, paid tribute to the hundreds of heroic firemen and policemen who died in the tragedy, got on with the work that had to be done, and vowed that New York would show the world that its people and spirit would not be cowed by terrorists.

TESTS BUILD CONFIDENCE

During the first part of World War II Churchill and Britain faced unremitting bad news. Hundreds of thousands of troops were evacuated from Dunkirk in the face of the all-conquering

German army. Britain suffered from relentless bombing. Ships bringing in food and armaments were sunk in frightening numbers by Nazi U-boats. There seemed every reason to be downhearted. Some politicians contemplated a negotiated peace. Churchill turned these challenges into a manifestation of the nation's resolve and an omen of ultimate success. Because Churchill could absorb and rebound with obvious confidence from the biggest setbacks, the whole nation came to believe that it too, could endure any reversal.

Consider Churchill's words broadcast on the BBC on June 18, 1940, just a few hours after hearing the devastating news that the French had capitulated:

> The news from France is very bad and I grieve for the gallant French people who have fallen into this terrible misfortune. Nothing will alter our feelings towards them or our faith that the genius of France will rise again. What has happened in France makes no difference to our faith and purpose. We have become the sole champions now in arms to defend the world cause. We shall do our best to be worthy of this high honour. We shall defend our Island home and with the British Empire we shall fight on unconquerable until the curse of Hitler is lifted from the brows of men. We are sure that in the end all will be well.

What a tightly packed marvel of hope and confidence! Churchill acknowledged the bad news, paid tribute to France, spoke of the noble task ahead, and made clear with the colloquial phrase soon to become one of his trademarks that "in the end all will come right."

Churchill understood the visceral appeal of an underdog and the inspiration of a fighter. Forced by the cheers in Parliament to pause in an early wartime speech when Britain was standing alone, Churchill added under cover of the noise, "And beat the b———s over the head with bottles! That's all we've got."

ADD PERSPECTIVE

Leaders put things into perspective. Churchill reminded his War Cabinet of all the resources Britain had at its disposal, including a dedicated air defense, a strong navy, and enough food. He was trusted because he never panicked in the face of a threat. Indeed, the British ultimately evacuated more than three hundred thousand British and French soldiers from the beaches at Dunkirk, ten times the number Churchill had publicly said was likely. In Parliament Churchill praised this "deliverance" but did not share in the exultation that it produced, pronouncing the evacuation a "colossal military disaster" and reminding his listeners that "wars are not won by evacuation." He did, nevertheless, find reason for hope and confidence: "This was a great trial of strength between the British and German Air Forces. Can you conceive a greater objective for the Germans in the air than to make evacuation from these beaches impossible, and to sink all these ships. . . . They tried hard, and they were beaten back."

Churchill's genius was to find a way to talk about bad news while finding hope in what others might see as defeat. He could put nearly any disaster in context. In October of 1940, after devastating air raids, Churchill gave a speech about how the cities "would rise from their ruins" and blitzed homes would be rebuilt "more to our credit than some of them were before."

Every leader could use Churchill's measured optimism. He saw the glass as half full, never half empty. He noted that the papers always ran pictures of demolished homes, but that many areas of London remained pristine. He observed that however horrible the attacks had been, by themselves they would not destroy the nation. Judging by the rate of devastation then current, it would take a decade to destroy half the homes in London, he estimated, adding with his usual verve, that "quite a lot of things are going to happen to Herr Hitler and the Nazi regime before 10 years are up."

Churchill had a gift for making the daily bombings or losses more palatable. When the Nazis sank vital supply ships, Churchill was there to point out that many hundreds of ships got through unscathed. He promoted a tone of calm amid the storm that many leaders would love to emulate. On the eve of the Blitz he directed that air raids be covered by the press and radio "in a cool way." His aim was to spread the impression "that the vast majority of people are not at all affected by any single air raid" and that air alarms and air raids should be treated "as if they were no more than thunderstorms."

REDUCE NEGATIVITY

As a wartime Prime Minister, Churchill had far more control over the media than most modern leaders will ever enjoy. While he was admired for telling it straight there were times when he held back news of a devastating military setback for a day or longer, recognizing that it might dishearten a nation already on edge. In mid-June 1940, for instance, Churchill was told that the *Lancastria,* a ship evacuating troops from Saint-Nazaire just before the fall of France, had been sunk and upward of three thousand men had perished. Churchill kept it from the press and radio. "The newspapers have got quite enough disaster for to-day at least," he wrote in explanation of why he felt the timing for an announcement was wrong. Churchill also rejected a request to allow American journalists access to British air squadrons to check the accuracy of figures on enemy aircraft destroyed, minuting: "We can I think afford to be a bit cool and calm about all this."

The message for today's leaders is that while you cannot control the media, it's critical that you set the tone and put things in their proper perspective.

Churchill understood that to build morale and confidence you must reduce symbols and signs of negativity. He dreamed up the remarkable idea of firing blanks when the antiaircraft guns were short on shells. Not only did he think the flashes on the ground would confuse the bombers, he felt the noise would "avoid a discouraging silence for the population."

Just as a company that appears rundown dispirits the staff and sends the wrong impression to visitors, Churchill would not stand for disarray, even during the Blitz. He ordered that shattered windows be replaced promptly in neighborhoods that had suffered limited damage, instead of letting reparable houses stand for "weeks deserted and neglected." He wanted gramophones in the air-raid shelters and was cheered to learn that one of his ministers had taken action on another musical idea. "I am delighted at the action you have taken about bands, but when are we going to hear them playing about the streets? Even quite small parade marches are highly benefi-cial." Churchill astutely recognized that music raised the spirit and he sensed that a soldier needs proper food to have the strength and the willpower to fight. He railed against "food faddists," dictating a minute to the Minister of Food: "The British soldier is far more likely to be right than the scientists. All he cares about is beef," growled Churchill. "The way to lose the war is to try to force the British public into a diet of milk, oatmeal, potatoes, etc, washed down on gala occasions with a little lime juice."

The same might be said for hard-strapped companies that foolishly cut back on free juice and coffee. Pinching pennies will not inspire your staff to work harder.

DEFIANCE AND OPTIMISM

A fuller sense of how Churchill spread hope and confidence during the war comes from reading his buoyant, defiant speeches and broadcasts. Read, or better yet, listen, to them and feel the vitality and thrill of that dramatic moment in history.

James MacGregor Burns wrote in *Leadership* that people who watched a film of John F. Kennedy's inaugural address "felt strengthened and inspired." Churchill knew how to make that connection and galvanize people. It's a quality every leader worth his salt would gladly give a few years of his life to possess, if ever so briefly. Future leaders should study Churchill's speeches for many reasons, not the least of them being that the sentiment and language is not only timeless but back in fashion. Half a century after the fact, many modern leaders facing crises still imitate Churchill's style. When Presi-

With Troops in North Africa

dent Bush and Prime Minister Tony Blair had to strike the right tone in the days and weeks after the terrorist attack of September 11, more than a few listeners recognized the style, if not the very language, of Churchill's most famous speeches. Even the latest books on business and leadership are filled with pithy phrases and exhortations that trace their origin to Churchill.

There are many famous Churchill speeches. One of the finest for leaders to study is his BBC broadcast on the evening of September 11, 1940. The Blitz was entering its fifth day and Germany appeared to be moving ships into position along the French coast. Churchill let his listeners know that invasion was possible, if not likely. He also spoke calmly of the historical importance of the days ahead and the opportunity for troops and civilians to rise to the task:

> We cannot tell when they will try to come; we cannot be sure that in fact they will try at all; but no one should blind himself to the fact that a heavy, full-scale invasion of this Island is being prepared. With all the usual German thoroughness and method, and that it may be launched at any time now-upon England, upon Scotland, or upon Ireland, or upon all three.
>
> Therefore, we must regard the next week or so as a very important week for us in our history. It ranks with the days when the Spanish Armada was approaching the Channel, and Drake was finishing his game of bowls; or when Nelson stood between us and Napoleon's Grand Army at Boulogne. We have read all about this in the history books; but what is happening now is on a far greater scale and of far more consequence to the life and future of the world and its civilization than these brave old days of the past.

Note how calmly Churchill dealt with the harsh reality of a possible invasion and the uncertainty of when and where the invasion might occur. Churchill provided the historical context that gave meaning and a sense of nobility to the challenge ahead. All too often leaders develop tunnel vision and forget that many people are terrified of change and the unknown. Leaders have to reassure followers, as Churchill did later in this dramatic speech on September 11, 1940, when he talked of the "superiority" of the Royal Air Force, the readiness of the army, and the strong fortifications of Britain's shores. Strong leaders always ask for something tangible from their followers, whether in spirit or action. The "commitment" section was a standard part of this and nearly every Churchill speech or broadcast. Churchill asked Londoners for "composure and fortitude" and to send a "message of good cheer" to the armed forces. "Every man and every woman will therefore prepare himself to do his duty, whatever it may be, with special pride and care."

That dramatic radio performance is but one of many Churchill World War II broadcasts and speeches that demonstrated his skill at balancing the facts with his unrelenting defiance and optimism. They are the heart and soul of leadership.

MAKE MORALE A GOAL

In the days before the Blitz, the Chiefs of Staff told Churchill that "the real test is whether the morale of our fighting personnel and civil population will counterbalance the numerical and material advantages which Germany enjoys."

Churchill made building morale one of the prime goals of his administration. During a crisis he was careful to take time to address his ministers or troops. During the desperate days of Dunkirk he wrote to his ministers and civil servants. He was not about to let anyone in his government think of defeat: "In these dark days the Prime Minister would be grateful if all his colleagues in the Government, as well as high officials, would maintain a high morale in their circles; not minimising the gravity of events, but showing confidence in our ability and inflexible resolve to continue the war till we have broken the will of the enemy to bring all Europe under his domination."

Churchill offered simple, pointed advice: the need to stay on course. This is an invaluable example for any number of trying situations facing executives or managers today. Leaders forge a sense of unity out of a crisis. This may sound touchy-feely but it is often what makes one troubled company succeed while another fails.

Morale clearly plays a pivotal role in the success of an enterprise. How can you motivate people who have every reason to be afraid? In the summer of 1940, as the Nazi invasion seemed increasingly near, the War Cabinet realized it needed to formally encourage the troops and civil servants. Every company or organization faces this at one time or another. Perhaps not surprisingly the War Cabinet first took the traditional but utterly wrong approach. Lots of drafts and approaches were considered and edited by many different officials. Churchill wisely took over the job, recognizing that no one would be inspired by a bureaucratic document. He wrote a simple, one-page exhortation about what each and every soldier and civil servant could do:

On what may be the eve of an attempted invasion or battle for our native land, the Prime Minister desires to impress upon all persons holding responsible positions . . . their duty to maintain a spirit of alert and confident energy ... the Prime Minister expects all His Majesty's servants in high places to set an example of steadiness and resolution. They should not hesitate to report, or if necessary remove, any officers or officials who are found to be consciously exercising a disturbing or depressing influence. Thus alone will they be worthy of the fighting men, who in the air, on the sea, and on land, have already met the enemy without any sense of being outmatched in martial qualities.

This may sound like harsh medicine but it may be the only prescription when the future of your company or organization is on the line. No matter how inspiring a leader may be there are some employees who cannot cope with uncertainty or adversity. They simply do not have the temperament to work for a company struggling to stay ahead of its creditors or scrambling to enter a difficult market. Leaders let these people go just as readily as they get out of unprofitable businesses. That, too, is a sign of confidence to those ready and willing to meet the day's challenges.

Every leader and company faces trying situations that test their will and confidence. The great lesson of Churchill's legacy is that he maintained confidence through so many huge disasters: the fall of France and the Blitz and countless losses on the high seas, in Singapore, and in the Far East. Churchill showed he could absorb these losses and the nation followed him, each time emerging stronger for having surmounted the challenge.

The goal is to remember these lessons when it counts, in a crisis. When an organization is fighting to stay afloat, so many other issues seem more important. But in the end the hope and confidence leaders instill are more important than the balance in the bank.

CHURCHILLIAN PRINCIPLES

- Make the creation and maintenance of good morale a daily aim. Impress on managers and workers the importance of a realistic yet optimistic outlook.
- Share the risks and hardships faced by others in your organization.
- Do not allow different standards for top executives and managers of workers.
- Develop an authentic aura of confidence and resolve. Trust, inspiration, and charisma are contagious and crucial in winning wars and customers.
- Regard tests as prime opportunities to build morale in your organization. Leaders realize that difficulties can be used to strengthen their character and that of their workers.
- Put bad news into perspective. Things usually get better, especially if a positive attitude prevails.

CHAPTER 11

Forge Alliances

When one looks at the disadvantages attaching to alliances, one must not forget how superior are the advantages.

—Winston Churchill, Parliament, September 21, 1943

Churchill demonstrated a keen ability to create and maintain essential ties and relationships throughout his career but he truly rose to the challenge in World War II, a time when alliances mattered. Consider what Churchill faced upon his appointment as wartime Prime Minister. A lesser man might have pushed for the leadership of the Conservative Party. After all, the Prime Minister of the day is usually the leader of his party. Instead, Churchill wisely chose to permit the ailing Neville Chamberlain to remain in that position, writing to him "as Prime Minister of a National Government, formed on the widest basis, and comprising the three parties, I feel that it would be better for me not to undertake the Leadership of any one political Party . . . I feel sure that by this arrangement the cause of national unity will best be served."

That gracious gesture (Chamberlain died six months later) helped earn Churchill the favor and allegiance of countless Chamberlain followers, several of whom he appointed to his cabinet.

STALIN

Contemporary leaders can glean much from Churchill's flexibility in forming alliances; none more so than the one with Stalin. Churchill had warned of the Russian menace since 1919, when the "bloody" Bolsheviks' "criminal regime" came to power. In 1939, when Russia had partitioned Poland with Germany and signed a nonaggression pact with the Nazis, he said, "Russia has pursued a cold policy of self-interest. We could have wished that the Russian armies should be [in Poland] as the friends and allies of Poland instead of invaders." But Churchill put aside his serious concerns when the Nazis reneged on the non-aggression pact and invaded Russia in 1941. He had no qualms about throwing British resources, scanty as they were, behind the Russians.

Churchill had a clear objective: the defeat of Germany. If Stalin could drain the German army's strength on the Eastern Front, all the better for Britain. That is why Churchill had no qualms about acting contrary to his past views on Russia now that changed circumstance demanded it. He displayed a decisiveness any leader might wish to emulate. To Parliament, having reminded it of his consistent hostility toward Communism, he declared, "I will unsay no word I have spoken about it. But all this fades before the spectacle which is now unfolding." To his Private Secretary he said, "I have only one purpose, the destruction of Hitler and my life is much simplified thereby. If Hitler invaded Hell, I would at least make a favorable reference to the Devil in the House of Commons."

The day following the German invasion, Churchill gave a rousing broadcast in support of Russia. Conscious that in the

CHURCHILL WRITES TO STALIN

Churchill wrote to Stalin after Germany invaded Russia in June of 1941.

We are all very glad here that the Russians are making such a strong and spirited resistance to the utterly unprovoked and merciless invasion of the Nazis. There is general admiration of the bravery and tenacity of the soldiers and people. We shall do everything to help you that time, geography, and our growing resources allow. The longer the war lasts the more we can help. . . . We welcome arrival of Russian Military Mission in order to concert future plans. We have only got to go on fighting to beat the life out of these villains.

eyes of the British people, Stalin was a despotic dictator, Churchill explained the situation: "Any man or state who fights on against Nazidom will have our aid. Any man or state who marches with Hitler is our foe."

Cultivating an Alliance

For some time before the invasion Churchill had been privately assisting Stalin with intelligence reports on the massing of German units along the Soviet border. After the invasion Churchill dramatically increased the sharing of secrets. The British had cracked the Enigma code being used by the Germans on the Eastern Front and Churchill ordered that Stalin be given selected details of German plans. With that timely knowledge, Russian generals were better able to counter German strategy.

Stalin was a difficult ally. Self-interest dominated any concept of cooperation and he was concerned only with what assistance, either material or strategic, Churchill could provide. As Britain was also fighting for its life it was impossible for Churchill to satisfy Stalin's demands. Stalin showed scant appreciation for the lend-lease supplies Churchill had diverted to Russia. There was no acknowledgment that Britain would be quite unable to invade the Continent for two or three years and little appreciation of British efforts in the Middle East, above Germany, and at sea. But Churchill persisted. Recognizing that communication is central to a solid alliance, he cultivated Stalin with strategic intelligence, news of British bombing raids above Germany and the campaign in the Middle East, and heartfelt praise for the valiant Russian defense of its homeland.

Churchill strove to make Stalin feel a part of events thousands of miles away. While in Quebec in August of 1943, after a visit to Roosevelt, Churchill arranged to have Stalin sent numerous slides (with a viewing machine) of the devastation wreaked by British bombers on German cities, to give "a much more vivid impression than anything that can be gained from photographs. I hope you will find a half an hour in which to look at them."

Building Comfort

A little more than a week later, Churchill congratulated Stalin for repelling the Germans from the Caucasus and Stalingrad (now Volgograd): "Pray accept my renewed expressions of admiration at the continued marvelous feats of the Soviet Armies." The following week in Cairo he told the press of the surrender of the German Sixth Army at Stalingrad, praising the "tremendous feat of arms performed by our Russian ally under the general command and direction of Premier Stalin."

Partners have a natural wish to be kept in the loop and be recognized for their efforts, and Churchill went to great lengths to make his distant ally feel connected. Churchill praised Stalin liberally in telegrams and letters. The strongest partners reach a level of comfort that makes a deeper relationship possible. Indeed, the fact that Churchill was so generous in his praise enabled him to be stronger in his criticisms.

During his first White House visit, for instance, Churchill found himself in the uncomfortable position of learning of a Soviet article that criticized Americans. He began his letter to Stalin with his "understanding" that articles in *Pravda* had "the approval of the Russian Government." Churchill continued frankly: "I feel you will allow me to point out to you the very great danger which might be caused here by a continuance of such criticism. . . . From the very first day of the Nazi attack upon you, I have labored to get all possible support for Soviet Russia in the United States, and therefore I must venture to send you this most private and entirely friendly comment."

Note how adroitly Churchill couched his warning in the framework of their friendship and privacy. Because Churchill had developed such an open, robust relationship, there was room for measured criticism. Stalin quickly wrote back, dismissing the article as unofficial and declaring that the intent had been in the "common interests of our countries in the struggle against aggression." He got the message. Future Soviet criticisms of the Americans were rare.

Perhaps the greatest lesson to be drawn from Churchill's alliance with Stalin is the importance of meeting conflict and bad news head on. By July of 1942 it was clear that Churchill would not be able to deliver what Stalin expected. No second front in Northern Europe could be opened to relieve the pressure on the Eastern Front. Instead, Britain would enlarge the campaign in North Africa. Churchill telegraphed Stalin with the bleak news on July 14, and the dictator replied angrily on the twenty-third. "First, the British Government refuses to continue the sending of war materials to the Soviet Union via the northern route. Second, in spite of the agreed communiqué concerning the urgent tasks of creating a second front in 1942, the British government postpones this matter until 1943." Stalin was furious. "I must state in the most emphatic manner that the Soviet government cannot acquiesce in the postponement of a second front in Europe until 1943."

Crisis Bonding

Stalin had failed to acknowledge that the northern shipping convoys had been suspended because of the catastrophic losses incurred during the light summer nights. He steadfastly refused to grasp the daunting logistics that the invasion of Europe would entail and the many months of preparation that would be required to make it a success. But argument at a distance would have exacerbated the situation. Someone had to soften the blow of this bad news in person.

Churchill listened to his advisers, who suggested that the Russian ambassador, Molotov, had "failed to interpret to Stalin the mind of the Prime Minister." A trip to Cairo was already planned; Churchill decided to add a Moscow leg to the arduous journey. His health was still uncertain, and he had to be tested with an oxygen mask (which was adjusted to accommodate a cigar) before the high-altitude flight to Tehran and then Moscow. He knew his task was formidable. Telling Stalin that there would be no second front in 1942, he later wrote, "was like carrying a lump of ice to the North Pole."

Leaders have to be tough, especially when partners test their resolve. But Churchill also had to hold his cards closely during his discussions with the dictator. When Stalin mocked some intelligence Churchill had shared, saying the Germans "were very good at giving false information to Allied agents," Churchill wisely resisted the temptation to respond. The intelligence came from German Enigma messages, and he could not risk compromising the source by acknowledging it to Stalin.

Throughout the meetings, Stalin often protested vehemently about the lack of a second front. He frequently insulted Churchill. Not only did the Prime Minister stand up to Stalin, but he calmly explained the military support the Allies were providing and as much of the future plans that he and Roosevelt felt comfortable in sharing, especially Operation Torch, the North African offensive. The lesson is that when entering into an alliance, it pays to stay with your game plan, no matter how rough it may be at first.

Upon the conclusion of the meetings, Churchill telegraphed Clement Attlee. "Now they know the worst, and having made their protest are entirely friendly, this in spite of the fact that this is their most anxious and agonizing time." Indeed, though Churchill gave as good as he got, his uncanny sense of human nature helped him realize that part of his job was to serve as a punching bag for Stalin. He let the dictator vent his frustrations over the absence of a second front, while convincing him of "the great advantages of Torch."

History has no doubt about Churchill's success. "If I were asked to give an appreciation of events, e.g. the visit of Mr. Churchill," Stalin said well into the talks, "I would say that this personal exchange of views has been of the most importance. The fact that we have met is of very great value. We have got to know each other and we have understood one another. Obviously there are differences between us, but differences are in the nature of things. The fact that the meeting has taken place, that personal contact has been established, means that the ground has been prepared for future agreement. All that is very valuable. I am inclined to look upon things with optimism."

Stalin's conclusion sums up what counts in a difficult partnership and what Churchill achieved. He made contact with a wily, stubborn ally and rose above major disputes to broaden their personal connection. Nor did Churchill have to give ground. In many ways it was his resilience and strength that won over the brutish Stalin. The lesson is just as valuable today as it was more than half a century ago. Strong leaders make allies of imperfect partners, while not sacrificing their principles.

ROOSEVELT THE ALLY

Despite Churchill's tough and astute handling of the Bear, an even larger challenge lay across the Atlantic. The Churchill-Roosevelt alliance was the greatest single factor in the Allies' ultimate victory. Modern leaders would do well to study how Churchill cultivated that relationship in what were, initially, very unpropitious circumstances. Consider just a few of the factors to be overcome. Churchill's predecessor, Neville Chamberlain, had insulted Roosevelt by rejecting his attempt to hold an international peace conference in Washington in the months before the Munich crisis. As the war began Ambassador Kennedy in London informed Roosevelt that the British would be quickly defeated. Then there was the rampant isolationist climate in the United States. Running for a third term, Roosevelt had to declare in September of 1939, just as Britain went to war, that he would make every effort to keep America at "peace."

Churchill showed how a leader can overcome daunting obstacles through charm, strength, and persistence. He managed to develop an intimate, unconventional relationship with the President when his nation was by far the weaker of the two and when nearly any sort of contact held serious political risks for Roosevelt.

The most pivotal, enduring alliances in business and politics come through relationships built up over years and decades. Churchill and Roosevelt had long admired one another from afar. In the 1930s Churchill had made clear his admiration for Roosevelt's New Deal and sent the president a copy of the first volume of *Marlborough* inscribed, "With earnest best wishes for the success of the greatest crusade of modern times." In a January 16, 1934, broadcast, Churchill praised Roosevelt "for the spirit with which he grapples with difficulties." Roosevelt, for his part, congratulated Churchill upon his appointment as First Lord of the Admiralty in 1939. The two men had much in common. Roosevelt told Churchill that during World War I each had headed his respective navy.

Once Churchill became wartime Prime Minister, he and Roosevelt began cabling each other much like modern contemporaries might exchange encrypted e-mails. But it was not easy going. First, Churchill had to convince Roosevelt that Britain would not succumb, as Ambassador Kennedy and others had suggested. He took a large step toward that goal in his famous "we will never surrender" speech after Dunkirk on June 4, 1940. Less than a week later, Roosevelt promised in a speech at the University of Virginia "to extend to the opponents of force the material resources of this nation."

Churchill's best wartime speeches frequently had two main audiences: the people of Britain and Roosevelt. Sometimes the most convincing argument toward building a partnership is what you say or do in public.

Hold Your Secrets

Despite Roosevelt's sentiments and words, the aid Britain desperately needed wasn't immediately forthcoming. Many of Churchill's advisers urged additional moves. In early June of 1940 Lindemann recommended "exchanging information" with the Americans in order to get from them some bombsights that "might make all the difference." But Churchill, angry at the lack of U.S. assistance, played hard to get. "I am still disinclined to do this at this moment. I am waiting for a further development of the American attitude."

When striking a difficult partnership, be careful not to concede too much too soon. Churchill continued to hold firm, also rejecting a suggestion that Britain pass on its radar and antisubmarine secrets to the United States. In a minute to General Ismay, he declared: "Are we going to throw all our secrets into the American lap, and see what they give us in exchange? If so, I am against it."

Churchill set out to get the maximum leverage from his advantage in strategic intelligence, minuting, "It would be very much better to go slow, as we have far more to give than they. If an exchange is to be arranged, I should like to carry it out piece by piece."

Modern leaders would do well to study Churchill's constant correspondence with Roosevelt. On July 30, 1940, Churchill sent "the good and the bad" since his last communiqué: "It has become most urgent for you to give us the destroyers, motor boats and flying-boats for which we have asked," he wrote, describing the new German ability to "launch U-boat and dive-bomber attacks" from the French coastline. Churchill spoke of how British construction of destroyers and "anti-U-boat craft" would come too late for the current battle. He described the severe losses incurred by Britain's destroyers: "We could not sustain the present rate of casualties for long, and if we cannot get a substantial reinforcement the whole fate of the war may be decided by this minor and easily-remediable factor."

Then came his request. Strong leaders never sound desperate, even when the facts are dire. They strike a tone of confidence. "This is a frank account of our present situation, and I am confident, now that you know exactly how we stand, that you will leave nothing undone to ensure that 50 or 60 of your oldest destroyers are sent to me at once."

Churchill was not asking. He was stating what was absolutely necessary for survival. "Mr. President, with great respect I must tell you that in the long history of the world this is a thing to do now."

Words and Deeds

Churchill's stalwart words were a start, but it takes deeds to cement an alliance.

On June 22, 1940, when the German-French armistice was signed, the French fleet had been instructed to assemble in various ports where the ships were to be neutralized. Churchill mistrusted this arrangement, fearing that the balance of power at sea would be tilted against Britain if the French warships fell into German hands. He advocated attacking the French fleet at Oran if they did not accept his alternative of putting themselves well out of German reach. Most of his War Cabinet initially opposed him but he prevailed. Two weeks later, on July 3, when the French rejected his alternative arrangements, Churchill ordered the attack. The majority of the French warships were sunk or disabled and more than a thousand French sailors perished in the five-minute action. Churchill's decisiveness in ordering an absolutely necessary attack against a nation that only weeks before had been an ally, went a long way toward convincing Roosevelt that Britain would not go under.

On August 14, an agreement was signed in Washington for the American manufacture of 14,000 aircraft and Roosevelt released to Britain the mothballed destroyers Churchill had recently requested.

The Careful Courtship

Roosevelt's campaign for his third term complicated the Churchill-Roosevelt courtship. Polls showed only 17 percent of Americans thought the United States should join the war if

London were bombed. In October Herbert Hoover urged Chief Justice Hughes to resign "with a declaration to the country of the complete necessity for a change in administration." Roosevelt's opponent, Wendell Lewis Willkie, seized upon a rare quotation in which Churchill had criticized Roosevelt's early New Deal policies. When Churchill verified the accuracy of the quote, he wisely decided to do nothing, saying "Less said soonest mended. Do nothing."

Delicate partnerships require a sensitivity to the public mood. Sometimes silence is the surest way to advance a relationship. Indeed, had Roosevelt's relationship with the ebullient Churchill become more of an issue, the controversy might have harmed the campaign of his American friend. Pledging "Your boys are not going to be sent into any foreign wars," Roosevelt was reelected on November 2, 1940.

Though the two leaders quickly exchanged friendly words after the election, relations remained sticky. Britain would have been bankrupted if forced to pay for the weapons received, but domestic politics still pressured Roosevelt to demand payment. Churchill had to explain the consequences of such action. He did so in a letter that even he felt necessary to draft several times in order to make his case with precision. Modern leaders sometimes overlook the importance of precision in communications. In the December 8, 1940, letter, Churchill not only described Britain's "strong and perhaps unexpected recovery," but documented its losses and the continuing threat. Most important, he made it absolutely clear that Britain was unable to pay what the United States demanded:

The moment approaches when we shall no longer be able to pay cash for shipping and other supplies. While we will do our utmost,

and shrink from no proper sacrifice to make payments . . . I believe you will agree that it would be wrong in principle and mutually disadvantageous in effect if at the height of this struggle Great Britain were to be divested of all saleable assets, so that after the victory was won with our blood, civilization saved, and the time gained for the United States to be fully armed against all eventualities, we should stand stripped to the bone.

These were tough words from a leader with few bargaining chips. But Churchill's resilience won him the next step toward a true alliance. Roosevelt was ready to seek a closer relationship and sent his friend and political adviser, Harry Hopkins, to meet Churchill. Far from looking upon this as a blow to his stature, Churchill welcomed his guest with open arms and began courting him in earnest. He quickly convinced him that he was certainly not anti-American and anti-Roosevelt, a view which Hopkins reported was held in some quarters in America. They passed entertaining and business-filled weekends together at Ditchley and Chequers. At a farewell lunch for Lord Halifax, who was departing to be the British ambassador in Washington, Churchill praised Roosevelt. In Scotland Hopkins heard a stirring speech from his host, and that same evening at dinner Churchill made clear his attachment to the British cause. Hopkins accompanied Churchill to Dover, only twenty-one miles from the enemy. Through charm and political strength, Churchill did more than win Hopkins's friendship. He won his trust. "Churchill is the government in every sense of the word, he controls the grand strategy, and often the details, labor trusts him, the Army, Navy and Air Force are behind him to a man," reported Hopkins to Roosevelt. "I cannot emphasize too strongly that he is the one and only person over here with whom you need to have a full meeting of minds."

The strong impression made by Churchill had an immediate impact. Upon departing, Hopkins wrote his host, "I shall never forget these days with you—your supreme confidence and will to victory. Britain I have ever liked—I like it the more." From this visit sprang plans for greater British and American cooperation, including the pooling of intelligence in "enemy-occupied countries" and the ferrying of U.S. aircraft via carrier "in case of urgent need." In less than a month staff conversations authorized by Churchill and Roosevelt began in Washington to consider the means of cooperation should "the United States be compelled to resort to war." Roosevelt arranged for the prompt sending of a Japanese encoding machine to Britain, the two countries began to act in concert, and in March the critical Lend-Lease Act was passed in Congress.

The lesson is that even great leaders should not disdain a partner who chooses first to send an envoy. By embracing Hopkins, Churchill won over a critical confidant of the President and advanced his cause.

Forward Momentum

In August of 1941, two months after the German invasion of Russia, Churchill pushed for the first of what would be several face-to-face meetings with Roosevelt. Throughout these meetings, Churchill was the protagonist, taking considerable personal risk to travel by ship or by air to the president. On August 9, 1941, having crossed the Atlantic on HMS *Prince of Wales,* he arrived in Placentia Bay for the initial encounter feeling surprisingly rested. One of Churchill's secrets was that he made sure to mix recreation with business on the voyages. He read a C. S. Forester novel on that first trip (as he would on a subsequent journey) and watched a number of films.

The meeting of the two great heads of state was dramatic. Churchill boarded the American cruiser *Augusta*, where he shook hands with the invalid president, who stood up for the occasion, supported on the arm of his son Elliott. The next day Roosevelt, his staff, and several hundred sailors and officers of the U.S. Navy came aboard the British battleship and joined its company for divine service on deck beneath the huge guns of the after turret. Although Churchill and Roosevelt had briefly rubbed shoulders during a conference at the end of World War I, this was, in essence, a first meeting. Leaders leave no detail to chance in critical first meetings and on this occasion Churchill even selected the inspirational hymns for the service: "For Those in Peril on the Sea," "Onward Christian Soldiers," and "O God, Our Help in Ages Past."

Churchill and Roosevelt developed an instant rapport. The meeting heralded several important advances: a joint message to Stalin pledging support for "the splendid defense that you are making against the Nazi attack"; expansion of lend-lease; the provision of American pilots for ferrying aircraft to Britain; and the Atlantic Charter, a joint declaration of war aims. Churchill's persistence and optimism, two essential qualities of the best leaders, were building a solid foundation for the alliance.

Yet Churchill still did not have what he needed: America in the war. On December 7, 1941, he was dining at Chequers with the American Ambassador, John Winant, when, tuning into a small wireless set, he heard the news of the attack on Pearl Harbor. With his typical verve and sense of timing,

Churchill immediately put through a call to Roosevelt to confirm the news. The President replied, "It's quite true. We are all in the same boat now."

Churchill seized upon the attack as an event demanding another Washington visit. Note how rapidly Churchill acted, how he propelled events forward with his initiative. He sailed just days later on the battleship *Duke of York*, and spent more than three and a half weeks in America and Canada. The visit spawned wide agreement on many aspects of the war. On Christmas Eve Churchill suffered what may have been a slight heart attack, but except for a five-day respite in Florida, his progress was not impeded. He certainly did not lose his sense of humor. While dictating to his secretary after a bath, Roosevelt came knocking, and in the commotion to greet the President, Churchill's towel fell to the floor. The door opened to a surprised Roosevelt, leading Churchill to famously (and truly) declaim, "As you can see Mr. President, I have nothing to hide from you."

While the amusing anecdote may not be readily applicable to most business situations, it's yet further evidence of how a nimble and animated Churchill was able to turn a potentially embarrassing situation to his advantage. Churchill, like all good leaders, looked upon these summit meetings as operas, demanding larger-than-life performances. And Roosevelt was impressed. His parting words to Churchill were, "Trust me to the bitter end."

CHURCHILL'S SPEECH TO CONGRESS

Churchill touched on his American heritage in his classic speech to Congress on December 26, 1941.

I feel greatly honoured that you should have invited me to enter the United States Senate and address the Representatives of both branches of Congress.

The fact that my American forbears have for so many generations played their part in the life of the United States, and that here I am, an Englishman, welcomed in your midst, makes this experience one of the most moving and thrilling in my life, which is already long and has not been entirely uneventful. I wish indeed that my mother, whose memory I cherish, could have been here to see.

By the way, I cannot help reflecting that if my father had been American and my mother British, instead of the other way round, I might have got here on my own. In that case this would not have been the first time you would have heard my voice. In that case I should not have needed any invitation; but if I had, it is hardly likely that it would have been unanimous.

The Human Factor

Leaders understand the importance of building human ties to help a partnership through times of strain. Personal meetings mean much more than other forms of communication. Churchill and Roosevelt saw each other ten times during World War II, at meetings that included leisure time together. After a meeting in Casablanca in January 1943, Roosevelt was eager to return immediately to America, but Churchill insisted that his fellow statesman and friend accompany him to "the Paris of the Sahara," arguing persuasively, "You cannot come all this way to North Africa without seeing Marrakech. Let us spend two days there. I must be with you when you see the sun set on the Atlas Mountains." And so they did, driving with a military escort. Soon after their arrival, Churchill insisted that Roosevelt accompany him up the tower of the villa where they were staying to gaze over Marrakech and take in the glorious sunset. In the morning Churchill, dressed in his slippers and flamboyant red dragon dressing gown, rode with the President to the airport to wave farewell at the airfield.

Churchill rarely permitted the pressures of the day to interfere with his zest for life. Meeting Roosevelt in Cairo, en route to a conference with Stalin in Tehran, Churchill made special arrangements to take Roosevelt on a personal tour of the Pyramids. Modern executives could learn much from these examples. Nothing helps along a partnership more than sincere gestures, meeting counterparts at the airport, or accompanying them to a special event. Churchill's enthusiasm and genuine friendship for Roosevelt helped bind the two men closer.

THE CROSS OF LORRAINE

Churchill admired the fighting qualities of the Free French leader, General de Gaulle, but once remarked that the heaviest cross he had to bear was the Cross of Lorraine, de Gaulle's chosen symbol for the Free French. The pressure de Gaulle placed on the Churchill-Roosevelt relationship is a wonderful example of how not to let a critical alliance get sidetracked.

In May of 1940, for example, Churchill had little choice but to reject the Vichy government, which had just concluded an armistice with Germany. Instead, Churchill and the British government recognized an audacious and arrogant general: "His Majesty's Government recognizes General de Gaulle as leader of all Free Frenchmen, wherever they may be, who rally to him in support of the Allied cause." But America, still at peace, maintained diplomatic relations with Vichy France. Nor was de Gaulle's cause in Washington aided by the petty intrigues that surfaced from time to time among Free Frenchmen.

Churchill had a soft spot for de Gaulle, who was also a courageous fighter. But leaders have no illusions about the faults of their allies, and Churchill was not blind to de Gaulle's shortcomings. "I could not regard him as representing captive and prostrate France, nor indeed the France that had a right to decide freely the future for herself. I knew he was no friend of England. But I always recognized in him the spirit and conception which, across the pages of history, the word France would ever proclaim. I understood and admired, while I resented his arrogant demeanor."

Roosevelt, with advisers in Vichy, saw only the arrogance. By New Year's Day 1943 Roosevelt made clear that in North Africa he would deal with General Giraud, who though not a

Vichyite had signed de Gaulle's death warrant. Churchill invited de Gaulle to his Casablanca conference with Roosevelt, but made clear that he would not referee what he viewed as an internal French matter. When de Gaulle balked at attending, Churchill replied harshly, "The fact that you have refused will be almost universally censured. My attempt to bridge the gap between your movement and the United States will definitely have failed."

De Gaulle went, fell under the spell of Roosevelt's charm, and by the end of April appeared ready to share political authority in North Africa with Giraud. But he foolishly delivered a provocative speech that blamed Allied troubles in North Africa on the Americans.

Roosevelt was furious about de Gaulle's inflammatory speech. By mid-May, Churchill was in America for the third Washington conference. Caught in the middle of the Roosevelt-de Gaulle row, Churchill was so frustrated that he telegraphed London, concluding, "I ask my colleagues to consider urgently whether we should not now eliminate de Gaulle as a political force." Churchill was right in valuing the President over de Gaulle but was saved from making such a hard choice. The Cabinet disagreed with Churchill, their reply informing him that de Gaulle was about to meet the American favorite, General Giraud, in North Africa.

Leaders listen to their advisers and Churchill listened to his Cabinet. From Algiers on June 4, 1943, he telegraphed Roosevelt, "The bride and bridegroom have at last physically embraced. I am entertaining the new Committee at lunch today, but I will not attempt to mar the domestic bliss by any intrusion of my own." De Gaulle and Giraud had agreed to become joint presidents of a newly established French Committee of

National Liberation, and Churchill wisely did not wish to meddle.

But Roosevelt was not convinced. In July he proposed a formula based on "cooperation with" rather than "recognition of" the committee. Churchill offered a diplomatic reply. Note the mix of toughness and flexibility. It is vintage Churchill. He asked the Foreign Office to suggest "a certain modification in your formula." And if that was not acceptable to Roosevelt, "we can talk it over."

In the end, de Gaulle posed problems for both Churchill and Roosevelt. Business alliances, too, can be complicated by third parties. The critical lesson is that Churchill managed to prevent the Frenchman from doing lasting damage to the British-American alliance and kept the de Gaulle-Giraud jockeying where it belonged, as a sideshow to the main event.

CHURCHILLIAN PRINCIPLES

- Put the interests of your company first, and logical partners and allies will become clear.
- Tough allies respect toughness. Stand up to an aggressive ally and you'll get better treatment and results.
- When striking a difficult alliance, it is crucial not to concede too much too soon. Leverage your clout and information.
- Strong leaders never appear desperate when seeking an alliance. They strike a note of confidence.
- Propel alliances forward with initiative and optimism.
- Nothing enhances a partnership more than sincere gestures.
- Leaders do not let critical alliances get sidetracked by minor players.

CHAPTER 12

Find Your Clementine

There is no doubt that it is around the family and the home that all the greatest virtues, the most dominating virtues of human society, are created, strengthened, and maintained.

—Winston Churchill, Parliament, November 16, 1948

I t is lonely at the top. Every leader needs someone with whom he can let down his hair, confide, complain, and discuss his worst fears and greatest successes.

This may be a spouse, a friend, or a colleague, but it is unquestionable that a leader is stronger with the support of someone brave enough to tell him when he gets it wrong and praise him when he gets it right. For Churchill it was his wife who fulfilled this role.

Churchill and Clementine had an extraordinary relationship. They called each other by terms of endearment, Pug and Cat, and wrote some of the most touching love letters in history, often embellished by drawings of their animal personas. But Clementine provided much more than emotional support for a world leader known for his bouts of depression.

Clementine was a font of political common sense, a loyal companion who never shirked from telling her man when he was getting something wrong. She also played an essential practical role, protecting Churchill from unnecessary distractions and intrusions and overseeing the financially overextended domestic scene that provided him with a comfortable and practical base for his work.

POLITICS

Clementine believed in Churchill and backed him unequivocally. In the political field Clementine's support for her husband could be forthright to the point of impertinence. When it became clear in World War I that he was about to be removed from the Admiralty she wrote directly to the Prime Minister: "Winston may in your eyes & those with whom he has to work have faults but he has the supreme quality which I venture to say very few of your present or future Cabinet possess the power, the imagination, the deadliness to fight Germany."

As a battalion commander in the trenches Churchill became bored once he had licked his battalion into shape. His mind sought challenges. He was frustrated, writing to Clementine, "Are they not fools not to use my mind—or knaves to wait for its destruction by some flying splinter?" The lure of politics was drawing him back to London. Clementine was anxious for his return to safety, and many wives would have encouraged such a move. Instead, she ignored her own wish to see him home safely and reminded him that his long-term success required patience. She replied, "I am so torn and lacerated over you. If I were sure you would come through unscathed I would say wait, wait, have patience, don't pluck the fruit before it is ripe, Everything will come to you if you don't snatch it. To be great one's actions must be understood by simple people. Your motive for going to France was easy to understand. Your motive for coming back requires explanation."

Clementine understood better than her husband that appearances and timing are critical in politics and indeed in business. More than once she reminded him to think of his legacy, to remember that however tired and tried he might be, he had a reputation to live up to.

In tune with sensitive issues, she often illuminated the best course. In 1921 the British government was beset by strife in Ireland. From a holiday in France in February she wrote to her husband, "Do use your influence now for some sort of moderation or at any rate justice in Ireland. Put your self in the place of the Irish. If you were their leader you would not be cowed by severity & certainly not by reprisals which fall like rain from Heaven upon the Just & the Unjust." Soon after this Churchill became a leading advocate for the reversal of British policy, which turned from hunting terrorists to a search for a lasting reconciliation.

PERSONAL AND PROTECTIVE

Churchill had a weakness for colorful characters of whose influence Clementine often, with some justification, disapproved. While she wholeheartedly endorsed his part-time soldiering with the Queen's Own Oxfordshire Hussars before World War I, she was less enthusiastic about the time he took from his busy ministerial schedule to participate in their summer camps. It was not the distraction from ministerial duties which concerned her but the well-founded suspicion that the opportunity for hard drinking and gambling was as much an incentive as the military training.

She was no shrinking violet. In 1916 Churchill was on leave from the front in France and had invited Admiral Fisher, among others, to lunch. The two had an extraordinary fascination for one another even though only eleven months had elapsed since

CLEMENTINE TO CHURCHILL, JUNE 27, 1940

10, Downing Street,
Whitehall.

My Darling, I hope you will forgive me if I tell you something that I feel you ought to know. One of the men in your entourage (a devoted friend) has been to me & told me that there is a danger of your being generally disliked by your colleagues & subordinates

* * *

mention it

Please forgive your loving devoted & watchful

Clemmie

Fisher's capricious behavior over the Dardanelles had contributed to Churchill's removal from the Admiralty. Clementine warned the Admiral bluntly, "Keep your hands off my husband. You have all but ruined him once. Leave him alone now."

Sometimes Clementine had to fill a universal need of leaders, the trusted associate who tells you when you're out of line. In 1940, soon after Churchill had become Prime Minister, she became alarmed that his temper and even his courtesy was suffering under the strain. She wrote, "My Darling, I hope you will forgive me if I tell you something which I feel you ought to know." She went on to say she was upset and astonished to hear he was becoming rough and overbearing. "My darling Winston, I must confess I have noticed a deterioration in your manner; & you are not so kind as you used to be." She knew he was under tremendous pressure, but wisely advised he would not get the best results by what she saw as "irascibility and rudeness." She ended, "Please forgive your loving devoted & watchful Clemmie. PS I wrote this at Chequers last Sunday, tore it up, but here it is now."

Ever alert to political nuances, Clementine stepped in whenever she thought Churchill might, in the heat of the moment, be misunderstood. Thus in December 1944, with civil war on the cards in Greece, she wrote, "Please do not, before ascertaining full facts, repeat to anyone you meet what you said to me this morning, i.e. That the communists in Athens had shown their usual cowardice in putting the women and children in front to be shot at. Because although communists are dangerous, even sinister, they seem in this war, on the Continent, to have shown personal courage. I write this because I may not see you till tomorrow and am anxious."

She was also adept at advising others who deserved to get

the best from Churchill. "Put what you have to say in writing," she told General Spears. "He never forgets what he sees in writing."

Clementine had a gift for making Churchill's important associates feel part of the extended family. To General Montgomery she wrote in 1945: "Winston loved his visit to you. He said he felt quite a reformed character & that if in earlier days he had been about with you, I should have had a much easier life—referring I suppose to his chronic unpunctuality & to his habit of changing his mind (in little things!) every minute! I was very much touched & said I had been able to bear it very well as things are. So he then said perhaps he need not bother to improve? But I said, "please improve becos we have not finished our lives yet."

One of the primary roles of a confidant is to tell you when you are overtaxed. Clementine saw more clearly than Churchill that sometimes he took on too many responsibilities. When Churchill was Secretary of State for War and Air, she advocated dropping one of the positions. "Darling, really don't you think it would be better to give up the Air & continue concentrating on what you are doing at the War Office? It would be a sign of real strength to do so, & people would admire it very much. It is weak to hang on to two offices—you really are only doing the one. Or again, if you swallow the two you will have violent indigestion. It would be a tour de force to do the two jobs, like keeping a lot of balls in the air at the same time. After all, you want to be a Statesman, not a juggler." Churchill generally took his wife's advice, although on this occasion he was right to continue with both tasks; no one understood the air as he did.

On other occasions he suffered from not heeding Clementine's views. She warned him of the dangers of speculating in the stock market in the 1920s, arguing that while he was expert in politics, he was an amateur in finances: "Let us beware of risking our newly come fortune in operations which we do not understand & have not the time to learn & to practice when learned. Politics are absolutely engrossing to you really, and should be & now you have Painting for leisure & Polo for excitement and danger."

Indeed perhaps the greatest lesson for leaders is the importance of taking the advice of your partner or confidant more often. Clementine, for instance, anticipated that Winston's loyal defense of King Edward VIII's courtship of an American divorcée would harm his political fortunes. During the 1945 election campaign, as the wartime leader of a national government, Churchill was visibly weary and not yet tuned in to party politics. He showed the script of his first electioneering broadcast to Clementine, who begged him to delete the insinuation that a Socialist government would "have to fall back on some sort of Gestapo." He did not, and it was thought to have lost a considerable number of votes.

In the 1951 election Churchill was returned as Prime Minister. Clementine had no doubt that he should have stepped down and let a successor into his shoes. She wisely did not want him to risk a reputation that could not be improved upon and feared for his health. Again he went his own way. It was a pity, as his age, seventy-seven, was beginning to show.

INDEPENDENT BUT LOYAL

Loyal confidants manage to provide advice and support without upstaging the person at the top. Clementine Churchill made her own mark through her personality but never at the expense of detracting from her husband's career.

Though celebrated for her elegant taste in clothes, Clementine was sensitive to wartime austerity. She made popular the bandanna head scarf style which factory girls wore for safety reasons. Arranged carefully at the start of a day, impervious to wind and weather, it was suitable for any event or function, from touring rubble-strewn streets to launching a ship.

In World War I when Churchill, as Minister of Munitions, was ensuring an ever-increasing output of munitions, Clementine was ensuring that there were an increasing number of properly organized canteens for the workers. In World War II she headed both the Young Women's Christian Appeal and the Red Cross Aid to Russia Appeal and even journeyed in war-ravaged Russia for seven arduous weeks.

The demands of World War II left little time for the couple to be together. Clementine, whenever possible, took the opportunity of a quiet dinner with Churchill, for which she always dressed in order to look her best. She was meticulous not to disturb her husband at work; urgent messages or matters which could not be discussed in front of guests were typed into a note or letter.

THE QUEEN'S RULES

Chartwell was Churchill's kingdom and Clementine made it abundantly clear that everyone understood the house rules. Churchill was king, she was queen, and the smallest act of disrespect was grounds for immediate expulsion. Once a cantankerous general repeated the old saw about how all politicians are dishonest. "If that is your view, General," Clementine announced, "you should leave Chartwell at once. I shall arrange to have your bags packed." The general promptly apologized.

She was proud of Churchill and told him so both in person and in countless letters. Fiercely loyal, she would not stand for those who sniped at him behind his back. And when her man was down, she literally stood in his place. In October of 1922 Churchill was bedridden after having his appendix removed. He dictated speeches to his shorthand writer, and Clementine, who had just given birth seven weeks before, bravely traveled to Dundee to speak for her husband. She wore pearls and did not flinch when women objecting to a woman's becoming personally involved in politics spat upon her.

In 1954, when a portrait of Churchill that was commissioned to commemorate his eightieth birthday turned out to be unflattering, Clementine made clear her view of what Churchill had euphemistically termed "a remarkable example of modern art." She had the offending canvas burned.

CANDOR

The secret behind their partnership was that when they did disagree they were candid with one another. The intimate trust that grew between them enabled Clementine to give frank and practical advice.

CHURCHILLIAN PRINCIPLES

- True partners tell you when you're out of line or when you need to take a break.
- Wise partners recognize short-term sacrifices must be made for long-term success.
- Able partners develop their own character and independence without diminishing your role.
- Loyal partners support and advise through good times and bad.

CHAPTER 13

Follow Your Canvas

What is the use of living, if it be not to strive for noble causes and make this muddled world a better place for those who will live in it after we have gone.

—Winston Churchill, Dundee, October 10, 1908

———

One of Churchill's greatest gifts to future generations of leaders was the example of his abundant love of life. Through every challenge imaginable and all sorts of weather, he lived life to the hilt.

Modern-day leaders could do worse than to study how Churchill relaxed and enjoyed himself. His extraordinary accomplishments were aided in no small degree by the fact that he seldom became worn down by work. Though Churchill worked with an almost religious fervor, he had an intuitive sense of when he needed a break or holiday. Painting, entertainment, rich friendships, and other pastimes broadened Churchill's horizons and gave him the pauses he needed during his furious daily schedule as a world leader and politician. The monotony of a nine-to-five grind would have dulled him. Indeed it could be argued that only by his system of making his own hours and interspersing work with diversions was Churchill able to achieve such breathtaking productivity. That's a wonderful, uplifting message for a modern-day leader: enthusiasm and inspiration come partly by finding your own rhythm.

MAKE YOUR OWN HOURS

Churchill relished responsibility, and it showed. At the outbreak of World War II, he was clearly rejuvenated by heading
up the Admiralty once again. His Parliamentary Secretary,
Geoffrey Shakespeare, later described how Churchill would
hold a formal naval meeting after dinner for a couple of hours,
then began composing his speech an hour before midnight.
He outlined his first draft with headlines and then forcefully
began dictating to a typist. Shakespeare was impressed by
Churchill's enthusiasm and sheer energy.

"Are you all ready?" Churchill began one nocturnal session.
"I'm feeling very fertile tonight."

As each page was finished he scanned it rapidly, altering a word
here and there, thus softening or accentuating the meaning. As he
dictated he padded up and down in soft bedroom slippers, arms
behind his back, head thrust forward, a cigar protruding from his
mouth. . . . Now and again he paused to ask me a question or I
made a suggestion. And he replenished his glass from a whiskey
decanter on the table. On he went. Crisp scintillating phrases that
next day re-echoed round the free world, came hissing out through
clouds of cigar smoke.

Churchill often dictated past two in the morning, capping
off the night with a visit to the War Room. But he was seldom
tired and rarely overcome by the astonishing pressures he
faced day in and day out. One of the reasons Churchill was
rarely bored was because he was so much more than just a
politician—he was also a historian, journalist, painter, brick-
layer, pilot, and host and friend to every imaginable world figure, including generals, artists, scientists, actors, politicians,

and businessmen. Though Churchill played a pivotal role in world events, he had the good sense to recognize what he couldn't control. Part of his energy and endurance came from his essential understanding that war and politics are unpredictable. Far from being sideswiped by setbacks, he often emerged stronger from adversity. "The element of the unexpected and the unforeseeable is what gives some of its relish to life," he observed, "and saves us from falling into the mechanic thraldom of the logicians."

Quite simply Churchill enjoyed the fray. As his Parliamentary Secretary recalled, "He knew from experience that war was a thing of hazards and dangers, disappointments and disasters, and was not unduly despondent when they occurred. He loved, too, the excitements and the tense situations which war always brings in its train. 'What a dull naval war this will be,' he said to me once with a spark of prophetic intuition. 'We have only Germany to fight. Now if we fought Germany, Italy and Japan together, that would be much more interesting.' "

During World War I, Churchill told his friend Violet Asquith of the thrill he felt at living and being a key player in such a great conflict. "My God! This, this is living history. Everything we are doing and saying is thrilling—it will be read by a thousand generations, think of that!"

Churchill lived his life with the certainty that he would be a model to future generations. That may be a lofty standard, but it can't hurt an aspiring leader to try. Indeed, Churchill lived every day as if it might be his last. He rarely allowed mundane toils to spoil his pleasures. Churchill may have often worked until the wee hours but he also catnapped when he could and nearly always squeezed eight hours of sleep into twenty-four hours, an achievement many modern-day executives might admire. Hitler didn't stop him from sleeping or enjoying a pleasant meal with engaging company. Churchill's prodigious workday might begin at eight A.M. and end at two the following morning, but there would be ample time for lunch and dinner. When he could, Churchill lunched with Clementine. At other times meals were occasions for Churchill to enjoy and often dominate the discussion.

After dinner Churchill often entertained his guests with a film before returning to work. He was probably the first world leader to begin renting films. His catholic taste led him to drama, comedy, and cartoons, and he had his favorite film stars, notably Charlie Chaplin, Vivien Leigh, and Greta Garbo. He watched old favorites, such as *Lady Hamilton*—about Admiral Nelson's mistress—over and over again. While crossing the Atlantic aboard the battleship *Prince of Wales* during World War II he showed the *Lady Hamilton* film to the ship's officers saying, "Gentlemen, I thought this film would interest you, showing great events similar to those in which you have been taking part." Newsreels also interested him. Frequently they chronicled events that featured him. "Look, Pug," he would say to General Ismay, "There we are." He watched films as entertainment, pure and simple, laughing heartily at the comedies and crying at the tearjerkers. Films provided a needed separation from the day's struggles. "The cinema is a wonderful form of entertainment, and takes the mind away from other things," he declared in one of his wartime letters to Clementine.

PAINTING AND PASTIMES

Watching films with British and American generals was one of the ways Churchill built camaraderie. Indeed, whenever Churchill visited troops, one of his prime concerns was making sure his men had ample recreation and entertainment. Churchill also found great pleasure and release from his troubles in painting. Today's leaders would also do well to occasionally immerse themselves in something apart from their business. Nearly every leader has a crisis or two in their career, and Churchill was no different. In the midst of World War I, when he was abruptly stripped of his authority, painting helped him to regain his footing and to dismiss the depression and uncertainty that momentarily gripped him. Not surprisingly, Churchill saw "audacity" as the first quality required in someone taking up painting in their forties, as he did. "The spell was broken," he wrote of his maiden effort. "The sickly inhibitions rolled away. I seized the largest brush and fell upon my victim with bezerk fury. I have never felt any awe of a canvas since."

Brightening a canvas with a pastoral scene along the French Riviera filled him with a sense of joy and accomplishment. He enjoyed the contrast between painting and his everyday world. He feasted on the "new mental food and exercise, the old harmonies and symmetries in an entirely different language." He had made the critical leap that so few leaders dare to: he recognized that he could become a better leader and man by occasionally stepping away from his cares and responsibilities.

Painting infused Churchill's travels with purpose. He had never cared for art for art's sake. Too independent to be a tourist, he suddenly found he enjoyed Europe's galleries be-

---

CHURCHILL ON HOLIDAY IN FRANCE
BEFORE THE WAR

He used to spend his mornings dictating to his secretary and his afternoons painting . . . His departure on these occasions was invariably accompanied by a general upheaval of the household. The painting paraphernalia with its easel, parasol and stool had to be assembled; the brushes, freshly cleaned, to be found; the canvases chosen, the right hat sorted out, the cigar box replenished. At last, driven by our chauffeur, he would depart with the genial wave and rubicund smile we have learned to associate with his robust optimism.

—Consuelo Balsan, Churchill's cousin by marriage, writing to a friend after Churchill's visit to her home in the south of France in the 1930s

---

cause he could see how the masters handled light and shapes. He gained a fresh appreciation for nature and found beauty in the "simplest objects." Painting sharpened his powers of observation. It may have also broadened his humanity. He once exclaimed at dinner that he had achieved every ambition he ever had save one. "Oh dear me, what is that?" asked Clementine. "I am not a great painter," he replied. However, already a master of so many arts, this was not something that really bothered him, for he was a very good painter, and part of his joy was that he approached the canvas without pretense. That's a valuable lesson. For talented, absorbed leaders there is something to be said for a pastime, whether it be fly-fishing, woodworking, or some other pursuit quite removed from everyday tasks.

Churchill lost himself through his paintbrush. "Painting is complete as a distraction," he wrote. "I know of nothing which, without exhausting the body, more entirely absorbs the mind. Whatever the worries of the hour or the threats of the future, once the picture has begun to flow along, there is no room for them in the mental screen."

Churchill understood the value of personal and professional rejuvenation. Painting, writing, and even bricklaying refreshed his mind and kept at bay his "black dog" depressions, deep valleys of melancholy that occasionally struck him in good times and bad. Variety is essential, especially for an executive. Churchill was invigorated by the intellectual challenge of writing a history or by the promise of a blank canvas. "Change is the master key," he wrote. "A man can wear out a particular part of his mind by continually using it and tiring it, just in the same way as he can wear out the elbows of his coat."

Churchill did not limit himself to painting and writing. He loved to work with his hands. In the summer of 1928 he helped lay the bricks for a cottage for his butler, built a large part of the wall for the kitchen garden, and constructed the Mary Cot, a playhouse for his six-year-old daughter Mary. "I have had a delightful month," he wrote to a contemporary, "building a cottage and dictating a book: 200 bricks and 2,000 words a day." He understood that the two activities were complementary. He worked his mind so hard that he needed to work with his hands.

During World War II it was unsurprising that Churchill had no time for his usual diversions yet he seldom lost his ability to calmly get reams of work done. "Winston certainly inspires confidence," wrote Major General John Kennedy, Director of Military Operations at the War Office, on July 17, 1942, shortly before Churchill began his epic journey to meet Stalin. "I do admire the unhurried way in which he gets through such a colossal amount of work, and yet never seems otherwise than at leisure. He was particularly genial and good-humored today."

Churchill's unconventional method of working played a key role in his achievements. He would start the day by working from bed; he would return to it briefly sometime during the afternoon and then carry on working well into the night. His extraordinary fluency in dictation also contributed to his huge daily output.

Churchill could compose an entire speech—or chapter of a book—in a few hours, accomplishments few modern-day executives (or authors, for that matter) can rival. Bill Deakin, an Oxford don, recalled that Churchill's most productive nights often followed a social lunch, strolls with guests through the garden at Chartwell, and, a warm bath at seven. He dressed for dinner and often entertained until midnight. The champagne flowed freely. Churchill spent nearly every pound or dollar he earned, and much of it went to support his freewheeling and generous lifestyle. As he famously told the manager of the New York Plaza Hotel in 1930, "I am a man of simple tastes, easily satisfied by the best."

Churchill's creative work often took place at night and frequently continued past three in the morning. "One felt so exhilarated," said Deakin. "Part of the secret was his phenomenal power to concentrate—the fantastic power of concentrating on what he was doing—which he communicated. You were absolutely a part of it—swept into it."

Churchill achieved so much at least partly because he knew how to relax. Without Churchill's hobbies and love of food, wine, and stimulating company, it's doubtful he would have been able to pack as much work into a day. Churchill loved holidays and spent many relaxing weeks in the south of France or on the yachts of wealthy friends. Holidays were occasions to work on his memoirs, to paint, or to lay bricks. When war came Churchill's recognition of the need for relaxation didn't diminish. Weekends at Chartwell or Chequers became minivacations, with ample social release and the simple pleasure of being surrounded by family and friends. Every leader needs a Chartwell, a place to ground himself in the storm and recover their buoyancy.

Churchill was never one to forget the importance of good food and drink in making politics and business go round. No matter the day's pressures he found time for a filet of sole or roast beef, accompanied by claret or champagne. Churchill's good humor and wit were often at their best when oiled by a little wine and food. He met everyone from Roosevelt to Eisenhower over meals, and business and politics were discussed at the table. A good meal never hurts business. Take the story of Churchill's efforts to reconcile the Prime Minister of Northern Ireland and the IRA leader Michael Collins. During a long meeting Churchill had arranged between the two opponents, he wisely decided food might help them reach an agreement. "What these two Irishmen, separated by such gulfs of religion, sentiment, and conduct, said to each other I cannot tell. But it took a long time, and as I did not wish to disturb them, mutton chops etc were tactfully introduced about one o'clock."

PLAY

Churchill's boyhood love of games and play never faded. He welcomed a good joke and used humor in every situation imaginable, including to humiliate Hitler. Wit was more than one of Churchill's verbal weapons. It was also one of the ways he got through a difficult day. He once said, "You cannot deal with the most serious things in the world unless you also understand the most amusing." Humor ran through many of his speeches, especially in Parliament, and like the best leaders, Churchill learned to poke fun at himself. Witness this aside to Lord Halifax early in World War II: "Asking me not to make a speech is like asking a centipede to get along and not put a foot on the ground."

Enthusiasm in a leader is contagious, and Churchill exuded it. There was something inspiring about the Prime Minister's taking pleasure from a dip in the Mediterranean during the heat of the war. Play and work were always intertwined for Churchill. At the age of seventy he challenged General Dwight D. Eisenhower to a shooting contest and struck nine out of ten bull's-eyes, beating Ike hands down. Then there's the celebrated after-dinner episode at Chartwell, recalled by an Oxford undergraduate guest: "Mr. Churchill spent a blissful two hours demonstrating with decanters and wine glasses how the Battle of Jutland was fought. It was a thrilling experience. He was fascinating. He got worked up like a schoolboy, making barking noises in imitation of gunfire and blowing cigar smoke across the battle scene in imitation of gun smoke."

Chartwell guests, too, often had to earn their keep. Churchill once challenged Professor Lindemann to "tell us in words of one syllable and in no longer than five minutes what is the quantum theory." Recalled his daughter Sarah, "It was quite a tall order. However, without any hesitation, like quicksilver, he [Lindemann] explained the principle and held us all spell-bound. When he had finished we all spontaneously burst into applause."

Anyone who leads for as long as Churchill did will have days and weeks when illness or accidents strike. But Churchill was famous for not letting sickness or fate interfere with his schedule. His stoicism helped him recover from all sorts of illnesses and setbacks. Just days after being hit and nearly killed by a car in America, he began an article on the subject. Later, in Bavaria, paratyphoid almost finished him off. Recuperating in a sanitarium, he started work on "The World's Great Stories," a collection of twelve stories. During World War II he was bedridden with pneumonia. The nurse who accompanied him on his return to Chequers was struck "by his immense vigour and enthusiasm, his determination to get over his illness as quickly as possible." Churchill told the young woman that he "ate and drank too much" but was much fitter than "old so and so who is two years younger."

The very qualities that made Churchill human and loved by millions—his passion for life and people, his love of painting, and his scientific curiosity—helped make him a better leader. Stimulated and refreshed by the diverse personal life he continually remade for himself, Churchill was both eager and ready to lead. What better example for future generations? One of history's greatest leaders rose to legendary heights at least partly because he discovered how to live and be a man in the fullest sense of the word.

CHURCHILLIAN PRINCIPLES

- Expect the unexpected and you'll find yourself far better prepared to deal with life's twists and turns.
- Make your own hours to bring vitality to your work.
- Leave time for rest and relaxation, especially when under pressure.
- Wise leaders have a hobby or pursuit outside of work that brings them joy.
- Never forget the rejuvenating power of a good meal with friends or stimulating company.

CHAPTER 14

Winning the War

In war, as in life, it is often necessary, when some cherished scheme has failed, to take up the best alternative open, and if so, it is folly not to work for it with all your might.

—Winston Churchill, *The Second World War: The Gathering Storm*, 1948

———

War is the ultimate challenge for a leader, and thus a study of Churchill's years during World War II provides an excellent summary of many of his strongest leadership qualities. Part of what makes war—and business—so challenging is its utter unpredictability. Try as you might, you can seldom carry out a strategy exactly as planned. You must do your best with the hand you've been dealt. More often than not, the opposition prevents you from doing what you would like to do. As Churchill put it, "An operation of war cannot be thought out like building a bridge; certainty is not demanded, and genius, improvisation, and energy of mind must have their parts."

World War II presented enormous obstacles, but somehow Churchill succeeded where others would surely have failed. He mapped out clear strategies and created effective organizations. He was inspirational. He chose talented subordinates and communicated his instructions clearly. Through it all Churchill maintained his enthusiasm and exuded confidence in victory. In meeting this supreme wartime test of leadership, he personified what this book is all about.

241

VISION AND STRATEGY

War and business are a subtle combination of setting and meeting short- and long-term objectives. The immediate aim in war might be to succeed in a particular offensive, the goal to defeat the enemy. But in business, as in war, it is no simple matter to get there. Long-term strategies are often complex and need to constantly evolve. "The issue, as is usual, was not in the realm of Yes or No," Churchill reflected on the difficulty of strategic priorities in 1944 "but more in that of More or Less."

No strategy succeeds without clear vision. Consider how Churchill saw the way through the morale-sapping succession of catastrophic defeats that left Britain alone to face a mighty Germany, which had already overrun Europe. It was clear that Britain by itself could not defeat Nazi Germany. But Churchill wisely judged that if Britain fell, America, still ill prepared, would also be at risk. The defeat of the Nazis demanded the active involvement of America, and this Churchill worked toward in every conceivable way.

This, in the dire days of 1940, was the long-term strategic view: Britain had to survive and persuade America that it was a winner worth backing. The strategies which ensured survival—the Battle of Britain and the Battle of the Atlantic—depended on other subsidiary strategies: the husbanding of fighters during the earlier campaign in France; the juggling of aircraft production; the courting of goodwill in Washington to ensure the supply of essential materials; the instigation of the convoy system for merchant ships; and the bartering of British bases for old American destroyers to increase convoy escorts.

Two critical decisions by Churchill helped persuade America that Britain was a worthwhile ally. The first, as we have seen, was Churchill's ruthless decision to destroy the French fleet at Oran before it could fall into hostile hands and tilt the balance of sea power in German favor. His second strategic decision saved Egypt, the Suez Canal, and the Middle East. Had Britain lost this crucial territory, America would probably have retreated into a defensive posture instead of sponsoring lend-lease.

The situation in the Middle East was the sort of crisis that makes or breaks a leader. At a time when Britain itself was threatened with invasion, there were huge risks in deciding to reinforce British forces in Egypt. But after considerable discussion with the Chiefs of Staff, Churchill decided in August of 1940 to back the effort. Virtually all of Britain's remaining tanks (and crews) would have to undertake a hazardous sea journey to the Middle East. Churchill advocated the faster Mediterranean route, but deferred to the navy's advice that this was too risky and agreed that they should go the long way, around the Cape.

Intelligence reports the following April pointed to substantial German reinforcement of the Middle East. Still more British tanks would be needed to defeat the enemy. This time the urgency was so great that the tanks went via the Mediterranean (with the crews sent by the safer route). The lesson is clear. Leaders must constantly gauge risks. Sometimes you have to put greater resources on the line to secure a vital objective.

Strategy is about constantly shifting priorities. "Everyone claims his margin at every stage," wrote Churchill, commenting on the margin for accident that is always a feature of military planning, "and the sum of the margins is usually 'No'." After weighing the importance of supporting Greece, which was invaded in 1940, against the danger of denuding the forces in Egypt, the Secretary of State for War, Anthony Eden, opted against Greece. Churchill overruled Eden replying, "Safety First is the road to ruin in war, even if you had the safety, which you do not." The forces sent from Egypt did not save Greece but they prolonged the campaign there, absorbing German troops which might well have tipped the balance on the Russian front and led to the loss of Moscow. The reduced forces remaining in Egypt proved up to the task.

ORGANIZATION

Without sufficient coordination, strategies flounder. Churchill had learned the hard way that a war cannot be run properly without the right organization. He had seen in World War I how not to run it. In 1914 the War Council met once a week under the chairmanship of the Prime Minister, who had no staff to brief him and no personal expertise. He was in the hands of fellow cabinet ministers who were each fighting their own corners. The Prime Minister had great difficulty in weighing one opinion against another and found it hard to initiate action. The Dardanelles fiasco was the direct result of this lack of coordination.

World War I taught Churchill the importance of effective organization. But the system had barely improved when he became Prime Minister in 1940. The armed services and government departments were each autonomous. The War Cabinet lacked clout, so that when strategies conflicted there was still no proper coordination.

Upon becoming Prime Minister, Churchill quickly appointed himself Minister of Defence, a post that had hitherto

Most Secret

BRITISH EMBASSY,
CAIRO.

Direction to General Alexander
Commander in Chief in the Middle East

1. Y'r prime & main duty will be to take
or destroy at the earliest opportunity the German-
Italian Army commanded by Field Marshal
Rommel together with all its supplies &
establishments in Egypt & Libya.

2. You will discharge or cause to be discharged
such other duties as pertain to y'r Command
without prejudice to the task described in
paragraph 1. wh. must be considered paramount
in His Majesty's interests.

W.C.
10. Aug. 42

A.B.
C.I.G.S.
10.8.42

not existed but that has ever since been seen as essential. With it went a small secretariat headed by General Ismay who represented Churchill when the Prime Minister could not attend the frequent chiefs of staff meetings. Ismay's secretariat kept Churchill informed of all defense-related developments, conveyed his instructions when they could not be given in person, and ensured that nothing stagnated. Ismay acted much like a clone of a CEO, always representing the interests of his superior, but not lacking in his own intelligence and drive.

Churchill was now in a position to debate strategy directly with the chiefs of staff and drive it forward. The lesson is to continually work to keep track of as many aspects of your business as possible. Churchill's able secretariat kept him apprised of every significant military development.

A constant dialogue developed. The chiefs were the military professionals, Churchill the politician. At high levels of command, however, it is not possible to separate the military from the political, and moreover, Churchill was not short of military ideas. He was by no means always right and although he pursued his arguments to their conclusions, in the end he would defer to military judgment, noting, "It is dangerous to meddle with admirals when they say they can't do things." In particular, the chiefs curbed Churchill's aggressive instincts when there was a danger of having too many pots on the boil at once.

Churchill also chaired the Cabinet and the smaller War Cabinet. For the first time in British history, political and military views were coordinated at the highest level and directly translated into plans that were promptly implemented. Industrial needs could be balanced against those of the armed forces. Men could be directed where required. The balance between the armed forces could be adjusted: when infantry personnel were in short supply in 1944, men were transferred from the navy. Steel and other materials could be apportioned between industries, to gun, tank, or aircraft manufacture, or to ship-building, in accordance with anticipated strategic requirements.

Churchill embraced all aspects of the war. He was still accountable to his Cabinet and to Parliament but he had acquired more power than is usual in the British democracy. He acknowledged this with the explanation, "This was really necessary because times were so very bad. It was accepted because everyone knew how near death and ruin we were." Just as battle-tested business executives manage to pull their companies together when they are nearly on the rocks, Churchill was able to mesh the military, manufacturing, Parliament, and the public in the face of disaster. As a colonel in Ismay's secretariat wrote: "The days of mere co-ordination were out for good. We were now going to get direction, leadership, action with a snap in it!"

Thus Churchill was able to bring together the Minister for Aircraft Production and the Secretary of State for Air to help him decide whether to reinforce the British fighter squadrons in France in June of 1940. Could the aircraft, if lost, as seemed likely, be replaced by manufacturers in time for the foreseen air battle over southern Britain? Churchill's reorganization made it possible to answer this complex question quickly. He decided not to reinforce the squadrons in France despite French demands. Anticipated future requirements and industrial limitations outweighed immediate military imperatives. There simply would not be time to manufacture replacements. British fighter strength, after further losses, would be inadequate for the defense of Britain. A less decisive response to the French request might have been disastrous. Risking additional fighter squadrons would not have saved the Battle of France and would have lost the Battle of Britain before it even started.

Leaders short-circuit bureaucracy. Churchill created a subcommittee of the War Cabinet, the Battle of the Atlantic Committee, demonstrating his understanding that in war he often needed to bring together representatives of widely varying military and civilian disciplines. The vulnerability of Britain's sea lanes gave Churchill many anxious moments. "I'm not afraid of the air; I'm not afraid of invasion, but I'm anxious about the Atlantic," he told the committee which gathered under his direction ministers charged with importing food and war materials, the quick turnaround of ships, efficient convoy routing and escort arrangements, and the rapid repair of damaged ships and port facilities.

The lessons for business leaders are straightforward. Someone has to be in charge and systems must be in place for authority to be exercised sensibly. Make sure to coordinate strategy and action. And autonomous or semiautonomous departments are most likely to thrive when they are in friendly competition for resources and markets.

STRATEGIC DRIVE

Formulating a strategy is an intellectual process. Keeping it going is about willpower. Churchill's hearty enthusiasm and pithy comments prompted action. When the invasion of Sicily was taking too long to mount, he burst out, "I never meant the Anglo-American army to be stuck in North Africa. It is a springboard not a sofa." When the amphibious landing at Anzio did not press inland as he envisaged, he protested, "Instead of hurling a wild cat onto the shore, all we got was a stranded whale."

Consider the position Churchill faced during the last week of October 1940. Greece had been attacked. The rate of merchant ships sunk by U-boats had skyrocketed. Civilian deaths by bombing exceeded six thousand a month. In one twenty-four-hour period seven hundred aircraft attacked Britain. Strategy demands initiative, even when the circumstances seem hopeless. The war would not be won by purely defensive measures. For the foreseeable future, the only way of taking the war into Germany would be by bombing. So it was that on November 1, Churchill pressed the issue, writing to the Chief of the Air Staff, "I have made various suggestions for increasing the Bomber Force. If instead of simply turning all these down, you and the Secretary of State recognized the need of increasing the bomb delivery, and set to work to contrive the means of doing so, it would be a great help. I beg you to let me have some further proposals of a constructive nature." It was an offer that could not be refused.

Military and industrial targets would be hit first. Bombing in those days lacked accuracy, and the devastating Blitz of British cities demanded a reply in the interests of British morale. Churchill pushed for area bombing, striking German factories and the homes of industrial workers. And he continued to press for targets of direct military importance. He ordered strikes against the Romanian oilfields at Polesti, the railway marshaling yards at Rome, and German rocket facilities at Peenemünde.

Churchill often expressed his strategic insights in deceptively simple statements, such as: "Battles are won by slaughter and manoeuvre. The greater the general, the more he contributes in manœuvre the less he demands in slaughter." Churchill was wary of immutable principles. His cautiousness was wise. In mapping out plans for business or war, little should be set in stone. As Churchill put it, "We often hear military experts inculcate the doctrine of giving priority to the decisive theatre. There is a lot in this. But in war this principle, like all others, is governed by facts and circumstances; otherwise strategy would be too easy. It would become a drill-book and not an art; it would depend upon rules and not on an instructed and fortunate judgement of the proportions of an ever-changing scene."

The same could be said about rolling out this year's model or introducing a new service. For your strategy to succeed, you need analysis and real-time adjustments.

THE EXPERIENCE FACTOR

As we have seen, before he became Britain's wartime Prime Minister, Churchill had held widely varying positions of responsibility in war: from junior army officer in India to First Lord of the Admiralty. He had also been a battalion commander in the trenches, Minister of Munitions, and Secretary of State for War and Air. Unlike many politicians, Churchill could talk on equal terms with admirals, generals, and air marshals.

Leaders need to understand the whole business. You don't need to be as knowledgeable in every department as your experts but you do have to be sufficiently well versed to comfortably air your arguments in a constructive dialogue. By the time

Churchill became wartime Prime Minister the job fit him like a glove: "I felt as if I were walking with destiny and that all my past life had been but a preparation for this hour and this trial . . . I thought I knew a good deal about it and I was sure I should not fail."

Beyond his experience, Churchill had studied military history, famous generals like Napoleon, and the campaigns of his great ancestor, John Churchill, the First Duke of Marlborough, whose life he had chronicled in *Marlborough, His Life and Times.* Business leaders do not have to write books but they need to know their business. The technicalities and details of an industry cannot be glossed over. The more you know about the history and intricacies of your business, the more likely you will be able to plot a strong future.

TACTICAL FLEXIBILITY

Flexibility and swift reactions are essential to cope with rapidly changing situations. When passing down your strategy, don't fence it in with too detailed instructions. Leave a loose rein for those charged with producing results. Only then can they exercise their initiative and react to changing circumstances without the need for further guidance.

Granting subordinates leeway in achieving objectives demonstrates your confidence in them. An excellent example is the clear field Churchill granted to General Alexander on August 8, 1942:

Directive to General Alexander Commander-in-Chief in the Middle East

1. Your prime and main duty will be to take or destroy at the earliest opportunity the German-Italian Army commanded by Field Marshal Rommel together with all its supplies and establishments in Egypt and Libya.

2. You will discharge or cause to be discharged such other duties as pertain to your command without prejudice to the task described at paragraph 1 which must be considered paramount in His Majesty's interests.

WSC

10 Aug 42

Brief instructions encourage success and succinct reports. Nine months later Alexander was able to report: "It is my duty to report that the Tunisian campaign is over. All enemy resistance has ceased. We are masters of the North African shores."

On the other hand, two years earlier, Churchill's directive to General Wavell had run to some four thousand words. But the situation had been very different. Wavell was responsible for North Africa, East Africa, and Palestine and had under his command a variety of Commonwealth troops who had yet to be incorporated into battle formations. Churchill had been in office only three months and was still licking things into shape.

Churchill has at times been unfairly charged with delving into details that should have been left to his generals. But in the main he dealt in detail only when he thought it necessary: when he noticed something that had escaped a general or when a military leader was getting something wrong or needed keeping up to the mark. His strategic directives were always to the point.

Churchill's method was often to ask questions and then suggest possible solutions, as in this vigorous, detailed minute to an admiral after a visit to a dockyard: "I wish you to look into the eight-day boiler-cleaning programme. How many destroyers are involved? How many men in each destroyer are involved? Is this special work for engineers or can it be done by able seamen?" After several suggestions the minute concluded with: ". . . so that the moment the destroyers came in the weary crews could walk off to their leave and rest."

Churchill's involvement in necessary details applied not only to his armed services. His personal appeal to General Eisenhower in 1944 demonstrates how wide ranging were his concerns: "Please provide from your vast masses of transport the few vehicles required for the Leclerc Division, which may give real significance to French re-entry into France. Let me remind you of the figures at Anzio [landing in Italy] viz., 125,000 men with 23,000 vehicles, all so painfully landed to carry them, and they only got twelve miles. Forgive me for making this appeal, which I know you will weigh carefully and probe deeply before replying."

Speed is a great asset in war and business. Delay hands the initiative to the enemy. Act promptly and you'll need only a fraction of the resources you would if you delay until the opposition has woken up. Churchill wrote amusingly on the subject in his war memoirs: "I have often tried to set down the strategic truths as I have comprehended them in the form of simple anecdotes, and they rank this way in my mind. One of them is the celebrated tale of the man who gave the powder to the bear. He mixed the powder with the greatest care, making sure that not only the ingredients but the proportions were absolutely

With General Alexander.

254

correct. He rolled it up in a large paper spill, and was about to blow it down the bear's throat. But the bear blew first."

Churchill had a warrior's sense of the fortune that favors the bold. Experienced leaders recognize that strategy needs to be swiftly executed. As the old saying goes, he who hesitates is lost.

FRONT-LINE LEADERSHIP

Just as a nation with good morale can survive all sorts of intellectual and physical hardship, a business with a contented workforce is more likely to succeed. High morale requires an inspiring leader. Churchill inspired with his words, but that was only a part of his leadership. Wise leaders position themselves where they can exert the greatest influence on the most important issues of the day. They are agile and spontaneous. Thus, in the summer of 1940 when the situation was desperate, we saw Churchill, in the space of twenty-four hours, walking the ruined streets of London, addressing Parliament, sitting at his desk working through the day's business, and broadcasting to the nation. He knew he needed to be seen among the bombed houses, to show the homeless that he was sensitive to their plight. He had to reassure them and discover for himself what needed to be done to help them. Parliament needed buttressing. The machinery of government needed the inspiration and prodding of his daily memos. The nation needed rallying.

Before the tragedy of September 11, some mistaken management gurus actually discouraged strength of character in executives. But Mayor Giuliani and other inspirational leaders have demonstrated that nothing beats leading from the front line during a crisis. A general who operates from the safety of his headquarters will never be inspirational. The troops are never slow to criticize such behavior, while the leader who shares their dangers is admired. This was never a problem for Churchill. He understood that he had to be seen and be accountable to Parliament and the common man. He relished leaping into the fray and had the confidence born of experience. He embraced dangerous journeys by sea and air, visited forward operational areas and was deterred from participating in D-Day only by the intervention of King George VI.

To lead from the front requires intellectual and physical leadership. Churchill excelled at this style. His communications expressed or prompted ideas at all levels, as we see from a selection of just five of the memoranda he fired off on a single day, October 20, 1940. A minute to General Ismay demanded "a plan for the imparting of more information to these very senior officers [the service Commanders in Chief]." To the Secretary of State for Air and the Chief of the Air Staff went thoughts on British bombing strategy, ending with "Pray let me have your observations." To the same addressees he sent ideas about night fighters while to the War Office he expressed his concern that the Polish troops were not sufficiently equipped, ending "I hope to visit them on Wednesday. Pray let me have during Monday the best possible proposals."

Leaders are not fazed by the technical. A prime example is Churchill's minute to the Chief of Combined Operations that resulted in the creation of the Mulberry harbors. These prefabricated piers (towed across the English Channel) solved the daunting problem of unloading large quantities of materièl on the open beaches of Normandy. "They must float up and down with the tide. The anchor problem must be mastered. The ships must have a side flap cut in them and a drawbridge long enough to overreach the moorings of the piers. Let me have the best solution worked out."

Churchill loved seizing on small details to boost morale. While visiting the invaluable code breakers at Bletchley Park, Churchill inquired how people filled their spare time. Upon learning that the great minds the Allies were counting upon to decipher the latest Nazi communications had no recreational facilities, Churchill promptly ordered the construction of a tennis court.

FINDING AND PLACING TALENT

When Churchill became Prime Minister he was able to start with a clean slate in filling political appointments. He obtained broad support by selecting ministers of all political hues. But he had no such freedom with the senior officers of the armed forces. Each had arrived in his position by the lights of his own service and the morale of the forces would have suffered had there been wholesale change. Indeed Churchill had no means of judging them other than by experience and that would take time.

Leaders seek able men and weigh results over personality. The case of the retired tank expert, General Hobart, is an excellent example. Churchill brought Hobart back to develop the specialized tanks (modified for amphibious landing, penetrating beach defenses, mine clearance, and obstacle crossing) to be used for the invasion of Normandy. Hobart was a tremendous success but his prickly manner upset some other senior officers and an effort was made to remove him on spurious medical grounds. When Churchill became aware of the movement he fired off one of his forthright minutes: "The High Commands of the army are not a club. It is my duty to make sure that exceptionally able men, even though not popular with their contemporaries, should not be prevented from giving their services to the crown."

Churchill, like the best executives, concerned himself with all levels of leaders and workers. Within weeks of becoming First Lord of the Admiralty in 1939, he strove to enable various tradesmen and men of color the opportunity to rise to officer rank. He wisely leavened his ground-shaking suggestions with humor, no doubt lessening the resentment his novel ideas might have caused among diehard senior officers. Writing to support his belief that commissioned rank should not be barred to certain tradesmen, Churchill asked, "Will you kindly explain to me the reason which debars individuals in certain branches from rising by merit to commissioned rank? If a cook may rise, why not an electrical artificer? If a telegraphist may rise why not a painter? Apparently there is no difficulty about painters [a reference to Hitler] rising in Germany." Churchill also shattered settled views on employment decades before the civil rights movements: "There must be no discrimination on race or color. I cannot see any objection to Indians serving on HM ships where they are qualified and needed, or, if their virtues so deserve, rising to be Admirals of the Fleet."

The talent and suitability of executives, managers, and workers are key to an organization's success. Don't leave employment and promotion policies to the "personnel experts." Promote from within before hiring from outside. And make sure that individuals can be promoted irrespective of race and color and, if suitable, from departments not normally considered "management" material.

CHURCHILL'S CHOICES

Churchill sought out commanders who thought and acted like him. Energetic men who moved instinctively toward the sound of gunfire. Churchill was frustrated by the lack of "get up and go" among the senior military commanders in the Middle East in 1940 and 1941. He had to move some senior commanders, though he abjured what might be called "hire and fire." Churchill preferred to fit the pegs to the holes. He rarely sacked a senior commander or officer, recognizing that even if justified it would likely sap morale.

Our story starts with General Wavell as Commander-in-Chief of the Middle East, with the 8th Army fighting in the Western Desert as part of his command. Early on, Churchill referred to Wavell as "our most distinguished general." But when the general became exhausted, Churchill moved him to India as Commander-in-Chief there and replaced him in the Middle East with General Auchinleck. Churchill was aware of the wear and tear that war wreaks on individuals. By moving rather than sacking Wavell he deployed the general's experience to better advantage. The same compassion and good sense should be applied to business executives who undergo extreme stress in difficult positions.

As it happened, Churchill soon had concerns about Auchinleck. The general became tentative and reluctant to intervene personally in the battle when the 8th Army struggled to survive. Churchill decided: "I now had to inform General Auchinleck that he was to be relieved of his command, and, having learned from past experience that this kind of unpleasant thing is better done by writing than orally, I sent Colonel Jacob by air to his headquarters with the following letter: . . ." The letter to Auchinleck ended: "I shall be very glad to see you at any convenient time if you should desire." Churchill told the War Cabinet that Auchinleck should not be "ruined and cast aside" and he later became supreme commander in Persia and Iraq.

When successive people fail it is worth considering whether the organization is a major part of the problem. Thus, when General Alexander took over from Auchinleck, the command of the 8th Army was removed from his immediate responsibilities and an appropriate general appointed to command it. General Gott was Churchill's selection but he was almost immediately killed when his aircraft was shot down. General Montgomery was then flown out from Britain to take command.

Montgomery was a protégé of the Chairman of the Chiefs-of-Staff, General Sir Alan Brooke, whom Churchill had promoted to that position after a succession of previous successful appointments. After recent setbacks to the 8th Army, Montgomery insisted on a satisfactory buildup before launching the attack at Alamein and relied on Alan Brooke to shield him from Churchill's impatience. Montgomery had another advantage that Wavell lacked. He was articulate and keen to explain his plans to Churchill, who wanted to know his latest thoughts. Montgomery's attack was successful, and with only a few hiccups the Alexander-Montgomery partnership went on to clear the Germans from North Africa. Alexander followed this with a successful Italian campaign while Montgomery went on to success from Normandy to the Baltic.

Churchill backed Montgomery because he was successful. He had an enormous ego and a tendency to rub Allied generals the wrong way, but Churchill wisely considered those faults a small price to pay for his brilliance in battle. Leaders aren't afraid of backing men and women who at times are trying or controversial. After the war, when Montgomery became the chief of the imperial general staff, Churchill described him as "Invincible in war, insufferable in peace."

Naturally, Churchill wanted results but he was sensitive to the many factors at play. "I have always followed, so far as I could see, the principle that military commanders should not be judged by results, but by the quality of their efforts," was Churchill's comment on a telegram from General Wavell following the fall of Singapore. Wavell had been sent suddenly from India to take command in the Far East and had written, inter alia, "I am, as ever, entirely willing to do my best where you think best to send me. I have failed you and the President here, where a better man might perhaps have succeeded." Churchill knew that Wavell had been set a virtually impossible task and thought that "Wavell's conduct had conformed to the best traditions of the Army." He replied: "We require you to resume your position as Commander-in-Chief [of India] to carry on the war against Japan from this main base. I hope you realise how highly I and all your friends here, as well as the President and the Combined Staff in Washington, rate your admirable conduct."

The maxim that "commanders should be judged by the quality of their efforts rather than results" may seem at odds with business practices, but it fits nevertheless. Sometimes the top man or woman for a job is the one who has made the best of a difficult appointment, not someone who has coasted in an easy position. And it almost goes without saying: you must be loyal to your subordinates.

Finally, in war as in business, nothing inspires like enthusiasm. Churchill was no warmonger. He had seen too much battle firsthand: frontier wars, the cavalry charge at Omdurman, and the trenches in 1915 and 1916. But he was enlivened by the rush of adrenaline triggered by his responsibilities: leading and lifting the morale of a nation; the huge task of organizing a nation at war; the forging of alliances with Roosevelt and Stalin; the dangers to which he often unnecessarily exposed himself. He relished every bit of it.

Business leaders could hardly do better than to study how Churchill led Britain at war. Generations of leaders have turned to study Churchill's wartime performance when faced with their own crises, from John F. Kennedy to New York City's Mayor Giuliani. Churchill was not a perfect military strategist or manager, but who else would have even stayed the course, let alone won, when faced with such a trial?

CHURCHILLIAN PRINCIPLES

- To achieve long-term objectives requires vision. Leaders adapt to changing circumstances and evolve and adjust short-term strategies.
- Initiative and willpower help carry an organization in a crisis. Remember that optimism and strength of character are contagious.
- Your organization must allow the selection and implementation of the best strategies. Make certain that there's ample coordination. And follow through.
- Leave a loose rein for those charged with delivering results. Give individuals the opportunity to exercise initiative.
- Speed is a great asset. Act quickly and you'll need fewer resources to accomplish your objective.
- Lead from the front, physically and intellectually.
- Position yourself where you can exert the greatest influence on the most important issues of the day.
- Engage yourself in the hiring process. Ignore perceived notions on the kinds of workers suited to upper management. Promote strong leaders, even if they are controversial.
- Be loyal to your subordinates.

Epilogue

Every one of us will be confronted during our lives with situations where we need to give the lead.

Some appear to be natural leaders very early on. Others develop the art as life progresses.

The young Winston Churchill did not shine at school. He was not captain of the football team or Head of School or even a prefect. It was as a soldier that he first demonstrated leadership skills. His confidence and authority increased when, while in South Africa, he took control after the armored train in which he was traveling was ambushed. As a result of his decisive leadership he saved many soldiers from capture and placed himself on the international stage.

Even at home taking command was a way of life. On seaside holidays he would direct the family party, his children and those of his brother Jack, in the building of magnificent sand castles. Everyone had a role to play under the direction of the "King of the Castle." He was as excited as the children when at high tide the sea rushed in to fill the moat and eventually destroy the entire day's work.

Although his energy diminished with the years my grandfather retained, almost to the end, his ability to enthrall his audience with wisdom, humor, and humanity.

I hope that his example will inspire you to rise to life's challenges, whatever they may be.

Acknowledgments

I am extremely grateful to Allen Packwood and the staff of The Churchill Archives Centre at Churchill College, Cambridge, for the enormous help they gave me in the research and production of this book and to the Master of Churchill College, Sir John Boyd, and Lady Boyd, for their support and hospitality.

My thanks go to The Imperial War Museum; The Winston Churchill Memorial and Library, Westminster College, Fulton, Missouri; Her Majesty's Stationery Office; Earl Alexander of Tunis; and Patrick Kinna for kindly allowing me to use material from their collections.

Most particularly I wish to thank Elizabeth Nel for allowing me to draw on her private diaries of her time as my grandfather's wartime secretary.

I want to thank Kenneth Houston Paterson for suggesting the subject of this book, Adrian Zackheim and Bill Brazell of Portfolio, and Denise Shannon for her enthusiastic support, help, and encouragement from the beginning.

Finally I wish to thank my co-author, Jonathan Littman, for all the spendid work that he has done to make this book a reality.

—Celia Sandys

I am grateful to Alan Littman for his assistance with the vast task of helping to draw insights from countless histories; I would like to thank David Placek of Lexicon for his generous reading of early drafts and his cogent ideas on naming, which led to our title, *We Shall Not Fail*; I appreciate the editing and guidance of Adrian Zackheim and Bill Brazell at Portfolio; as always, I value the support of Kristine Dahl.

I wish to thank Celia Sandys for the rare opportunity to collaborate in this work about her grandfather. Most of all, I would like to thank Winston Churchill himself, for a life filled with strength and character that has been an inspiration even as I attempted in a small way to do it justice.

—Jonathan Littman

Index

The Churchill Centre and Societies

(www.winstonchurchill.org)

Celia Sandys is pleased to be a Trustee of The Churchill Centre and strongly recommends membership to anyone interested in Winston Churchill.

Headquartered in Washington, D.C., and active internationally, The Churchill Centre was founded in 1968 to inspire leadership, statesmanship, vision, and boldness among democratic and freedom-loving peoples through the thoughts, words, works, and deeds of Winston Spencer Churchill. Membership numbers more than three thousand, with an average age of forty-eight, including the affiliated Churchill Societies of the UK and Canada.

The Churchill Centre publishes a quarterly magazine, *Finest Hour;* a newsletter, the *Chartwell Bulletin;* and periodic collections of papers and speeches, the *Churchill Proceedings.* It sponsors international and national conferences and Churchill tours, which have visited Britain, Australia, France, South Africa, and Morocco. Its expansive Web site, www.winston churchill.org, now includes a "classroom" component to help educate young people on Sir Winston's life and leadership.

The Churchill Centre has helped bring about republication of more than twenty of Winston Churchill's long-out-of-print books. In 1992, it launched a campaign for completion of the remaining document volumes to the official biography, three of which have been published to date. More recently, it sponsored academic symposia in America and Britain; seminars where students and scholars discuss Churchill's books; scholarships for Churchill Studies at the universities of Edinburgh and Dallas; and important reference works. In 1998, it launched the Churchill Lecture Series, in which prominent world figures apply Sir Winston's experience to the world today.

In 2003, The Churchill Centre opened its first official headquarters in Washington, D.C., which houses its administrative staff, library, and computer facilities linked to the major Churchill archives. Future programs include video aids for schoolchildren; college- and graduate-level courses on aspects of Churchill's career; fellowships to assist students; and visiting professorships. The overall aim is to impress Churchill's qualities of leadership firmly on the leaders of the twenty-first century.

Membership in The Churchill Centre and Societies is available for a modest subscription, with special rates for students. For further information, please contact:

The Churchill Centre
Suite 312
1750 17th Street N.W.
Washington, D.C. 20002
Telephone: (888) WSC-1874
Web site: www.winstonchurchill.org

International Churchill Society
P.O. Box 1257
Melksham Wilts.
England SN12 6GQ
Telephone: (01380) 828609

International Churchill Society
3256 Rymal Road
Mississauga Ontario
Canada L4Y 3CI
Telephone: (905) 279-5169